Bruce R. & Sharon W.
Short
TEDS Winter 1980

TOWARD

NEW

HORIZONS

TOWARD

NEW

HORIZONS

DR. ROY A. THOMPSON

Dynamic Developments in the Evangelical
Free Church of America in the decade
following the Diamond Jubilee, 1959-1969

Free Church Publications

Minneapolis, Minnesota

Standard Book Number 911802-22-3

Library of Congress Catalog Card Number 73-86579

Printed in the United States of America
Free Church Press

President of the Evangelical Free Church of America, Dr. Arnold T. Olson, with Congressman Elford A. Cederberg, a member of our Bay City, Michigan congregation, make the 1959 presentation of the *Diamond Jubilee Story* to the President of the United States, Dwight D. Eisenhower. Cederberg, the first Free Church member to serve in the U.S. Congress, is now a veteran legislator serving his ninth term, and is joined by a member of the Rockford, Ill. First Free Church, Congressman John B. Anderson, recently reelected to his fifth term.

FOREWORD

Among the many names which have been suggested for the period, 1960-1970, is "Decade of Acceleration."

There has been a speed-up in travel, in communications, in the acquiring of knowledge, in our ways of doing things, in finding cures for diseases, to say nothing about what computers have done to the making of and reporting statistics and calculations. As one reads this volume, he will sense not only the growth of the church during this decade but the acceleration of that increase.

In presenting the history of the first 75 years to President Dwight David Eisenhower in the oval room at the White House on June 14, 1959, I said, "This book tells of the contribution made by a small group of immigrants to the religious life of America. It is also a report on what the second and third generations have done with that heritage." Reflecting on it later, I wrote, "Symbolically, it represented a report to our nation on what our fathers have done. How wonderful to know it could be done with pride."

"Toward New Horizons," however, tells of what we, by God's grace, have been able to accomplish. May we read it in a spirit of gratitude and rededication.

Arnold Theodore Olson

Minneapolis, Minnesota

April 9, 1969

The dynamic decade from the Diamond Jubilee Conference in 1959 to the 85th anniversary conference of the Evangelical Free Church of America in 1969 is highlighted in these pages. The title chosen, *Toward New Horizons,* fittingly recognizes a truth shared in Dr. Arnold Olson's presidential challenge on the eve of the Diamond Jubilee year, that *". . . we are not on a pilgrimage to the shrines of yesterday. We are on a crusade to plant flags in new territories for Christ. We have not yet caught up with our horizons."*

We have been trying to catch up with our horizons during the past decade. We dare not say we have done so. We may say, however, that there has been a strong desire to emulate the Apostle Paul's attitude, who said, "I do not claim that I have already succeeded in this, or have already become perfect. I keep going on to try to possess it . . . and run straight toward the goal in order to win the prize." (Phil. 3:12-14, Today's English Version).

The *Diamond Jubilee Story* records considerable progress toward new horizons up to that climactic 75th anniversary year. Since then, however, the *rate* of advance has accelerated as we have witnessed the founding of a college in Canada, the Golden Anniversary celebration of our Canadian work climaxed by the receipt of a Dominion Charter by the newly organized Evangelical Free Church of Canada, the phenomenal growth of Trinity College and Trinity Evangelical Divinity School, the building of a hospital and new children's home in Hong Kong, the new Headquarters building in Minneapolis, and the ever-widening outreach of EFCA influence around the world.

The story of what God has wrought during the past ten years provides no occasion for self-congratulation or complacency.

There is much for which there should be genuine and deep gratitude to God for what has been accomplished through the dedicated efforts of dedicated men and women working together for God's glory and the advancement of His kingdom. But the story should also constitute a challenge to pray more, to give more, to work harder, so that we might come a little closer to "catching up with our horizons."

—Roy A. Thompson

CONTENTS

ONE

DIAMOND JUBILEE STORY

THE FIRST SEVENTY-FIVE YEARS

Ten years have passed since the publishing of the 335-page *Diamond Jubilee Story* unveiling the history of the first 75 years of the Evangelical Free Church. We now pick up the threads of that thrilling record of our heritage to weave again a colorful addition covering the last ten years, in which our work has marched steadfastly forward *toward new horizons.* It is fitting that we begin with a brief review of the *Diamond Jubilee Story.* This will serve as a stimulating refresher course for those who have already read it, and a vital briefing for the new soldiers of the Cross in our ranks, to enable them to keep in step as we continue the *crusade to plant flags in new territories for Christ* and to step up the effort to *catch up with our horizons.*

Here, then, are the highlights of the five sections comprising the *Diamond Jubilee Story.* Part I of that book, written by Dr. H. Wilbert Norton, traces the development of the "free church movement" from apostolic times. Part II, written by the Rev. Olai Urang, describes the origin and development of the Evangelical

Free Church Association—the Norwegian-Danish group. Part III, written by the present writer, does the same for the Evangelical Free Church of America—the former Swedish group. The story of the merger of the two groups constitutes Part IV, and the nine years following the merger, written by Mel Larson, are described in Part V.

PART I. THE DEVELOPMENT OF THE FREE CHURCH MOVEMENT

Dr. Norton traces the history of "free and evangelical" churches and church groups from the very beginning of the Christian Era. His fifty pages of excellent material are an elaboration of the first sentence of his treatise, namely, that "The founding of the Evangelical Free Church of America in 1884 marked a new phase of a movement in the history of the Christian Church which is as old as the Church itself."

He calls attention to the fact that the local churches established in Jerusalem, Antioch, Ephesus, Corinth, Rome, Philippi, Colosse, Thessalonica, etc. were not only *evangelical* groups composed of believers only, but were also *free* from any ecclesiastical domination such as characterized the established or institutional churches of a later period.

Referring to a scholarly work by the great Swedish historian, Prof. Gunnar Westin, entitled *The Free Church Through the Ages,"* he describes the tensions and conflicts between the "free church movement" and the institutional church from the second century on. Though some of these movements might not be considered strictly orthodox from our point of view, they were really "free church movements" though called by other names, such as Marcionism, Montanism, Donatism, Novatianism, etc., in that they opposed the established Church and emphasized the authority of the Scriptures and a pure and regenerate church membership, as well as the autonomy of the local church.

There were also pre-Reformation movements such as the Waldensian church, Lollardism (under the leadership of John Wycliffe), and the Hussite movement, which maintained these same principles in spite of great opposition and persecution by the established Church.

The Protestant Reformation did not accelerate the development of the free church movement, as one might suppose. The popular leaders of the Reformation—Luther, Zwingli, and Calvin—were advocates of State churches and resisted such free church movements as the Anabaptists, Hutterites and Mennonites, and later the Congregationalists. Persecution of the free church leaders continued with little abatement. Some of the leaders were actually put to death for holding and advocating the principles that are so precious to us today, such as a pure regenerate church membership and the authority of the Scriptures.

The Lutheran State Churches of the Scandinavian countries following the Reformation did their best to stamp out the "free church movement" that had spread from other European countries where the preaching of the Gospel in its simplicity had brought spiritual revival to many communities. The governments of these countries tried in vain to prevent the Bible-believing Christians from having their own gatherings for worship and the observance of the Lord's Supper. Such prohibitions only fanned into a brighter flame the spirit of revival and the determination of the believers to resist the established Church and maintain their principle of freedom. The last half of the 19th century witnessed the formation of several free church denominations, including the Methodist and Baptist Churches and the Mission Covenant Churches of these countries.

Throughout Europe the free church movement has continued to make its influence felt, especially during the past one hundred years, as Dr. Arnold Olson has pointed out in *Believers Only*. Historians have characterized this segment of Protestantism as "the left-wing of Protestantism," the right wing being those churches that have been established by law as State religions. These "left-wing" groups have persisted and grown in spite of the legal restrictions imposed on them by their governments. It is only during the last few decades that religious freedom has been granted to most of these churches, and some of them are still without that freedom.

The story of these free and independent evangelical groups in Europe and how they discovered one another and established the International Federation of Free Evangelical Churches is reported in a fascinating manner in Dr. Olson's book.

These groups are found in Switzerland, Germany, France, the Netherlands, Czechoslovakia, Norway, Sweden, Denmark, Finland, Greece, and Spain. The Evangelical Free Church of America and the Evangelical Covenant Churches of the United States and Canada are affiliated with these European churches in the International Federation.

It was the immigrants from Europe—the Scandinavian countries in particular—during the last three decades of the 19th century and the early part of the 20th century—men and women saved in the revivals of those lands and imbued with this "free church spirit"—who were used of the Lord in the formation of what has become The Evangelical Free Church of America.

PART II. THE ORIGIN AND DEVELOPMENT OF THE EVANGELICAL FREE CHURCH ASSOCIATION

The Norwegian-Danish Evangelical Free Church Association "started with a group of isolated outposts rather than with a concerted offensive," as Mr. Urang points out at the beginning of this section of the *Diamond Jubilee Story*. The immigrants from Norway and Denmark had been part of a similar spiritual movement there. Coming to this country they would naturally seek the same kind of fellowship in their new communities.

Three separate events, all taking place in the year 1884, might be said to have influenced the formation of the Norwegian-Danish Evangelical Free Church Association. There was the establishment of the Norwegian-Danish Institute at the Chicago Theological Seminary by the Rev. P. C. Trandberg of Bornholm, Denmark.

This proved to be a kind of rallying point for the Norwegian and Danish Christians in the Chicago area. Some of the young men who attended the Institute became leaders in the formation and development of the Association.

A mighty revival that came to Oslo, Norway, through the preaching of the Rev. Fredrik Franson and the founding of the Bethlehem church there is also considered to have influenced the launching of the Association, since converts coming from Oslo added to the number of Norwegian and Danish Christians who were seeking an opportunity for worship and fellowship with their fellow-countrymen.

Also, during the same year, the first Norwegian-Danish Evangelical Free Church in the United States was organized, in Boston, Mass., when seven believers came together for that purpose.

Subsequently similar groups were formed in Iowa, Michigan, New Jersey, New York, Connecticut, Wisconsin and other places. As these groups learned to know each other the desire for fellowship and cooperation would lead eventually to the formation of organized associations.

What was needed to bring this about was a publication, and this was launched in 1889, called *Evangelisten* (The Evangelist). It is significant that within two years after the launching of the paper, a meeting was called at Salem Free Church in Chicago for the purpose of organizing the churches of the Midwest into an association. There was some disagreement as to what to call the organization, some of them urging that it be called the Western District of the Evangelical Free Church, others feeling that the word "Congregational" should be included in the name. Mr. Urang said they compromised by calling it The Western Evangelical Free Church Association (Cong.). The "compromise" might be thought rather one-sided since the word "Congregational" was not only abbreviated but put in parentheses!

A little later the same year (1891) Dr. R. A. Jernberg, at that time president of the Norwegian-Danish Institute, helped the

Eastern churches organize the Eastern Evangelical Free Church Association.

The organization of the associations gave new impetus to the churches, which began to consider, at their conferences, such questions as "How can we interest our churches in home missions?" "How can we spread the Free Church movement in this country?" and "How can we give our children a systematic Christian education?" In 1896 a Scandinavian missionary society was organized to promote home missions. It had the cumbersome name of The Eastern Norwegian-Danish Free Church Itinerant Preachers' Movement.

Foreign missions, too, was promoted with great enthusiasm at this time. Inspired by world missionary Fredrik Franson, the Rev. C. T. Dyrness of Salem Free Church, Chicago; Dr. O. C. Grauer of the Norwegian-Danish Institute and others assisted Mr. Franson in organizing the Scandinavian Alliance Mission (now known as TEAM, or The Evangelical Alliance Mission), and channeled their missionary work through that organization.

For several years after the formation of the Western and Eastern associations, efforts were made to unite the two groups into a national organization. These efforts finally proved successful when the two associations at their annual meetings adopted a resolution of merger in May of 1909. A confession of faith was also adopted at that time, though not without some vigorous opposition. Dr. Jernberg, unable to attend the meeting, wrote to the conference, "For twenty-five years we have existed without a confession of faith, and why should we have need of it now?" Incorporation did not take place until 1912.

An incentive for the two associations to merge was the offer of a school building at Rushford, Minn. that would enable the Association to establish its own Bible Institute and Academy. With Dr. L. J. Pedersen as president and the principal teacher, and Miss Grace Skow of Wesley, Iowa (Mrs. E. M. Paulson) assisting, the school opened its doors with the two teachers and 19 students on September 28, 1910.

A still more suitable property for developing the school work was made available in 1916, when the school moved to Minneapolis, close to the University of Minnesota. Enthusiasm was high as enrollment during the first fall in the new location jumped to 62.

Meanwhile the tie with the Norwegian-Danish Institute was being gradually dissolved.

Though the principal concern of the churches was that of carrying out the Great Commission and the training of men and women for that work, the social implications of the Gospel were not ignored. Several benevolent institutions were established during the early part of this century, namely, the Christian Home for Children at Fort Lee, New Jersey; the Norwegian Christian Home for the Aged in Brooklyn; the Lydia Children's Home in Chicago; also homes for girls in Boston, Brooklyn and Chicago. A Ministerial Pension Fund was also established in 1919 to provide a small measure of financial assistance to needy or retired pastors.

Following World War I the churches faced the difficult language problem. A generation of young people were demanding a change from Norwegian to English in the Sunday school and worship services. The wave of immigration from the old country had subsided and the churches began to realize that there could be no future for their work unless they were willing to make the transition from Norwegian to English. They could no longer afford to be concerned only with reaching fellow-Norwegians or fellow-Danes with the Gospel but must reach out to the needy souls in their own communities who could not be reached by means of a foreign language.

Numerical growth during these transition days was negligible, but the work as a whole was becoming better organized and foundations were being laid for a period of expansion following the Depression of the 30's.

No doubt the brightest aspect of the united work during the depression years was the expansion of the Free Church work in

Canada. The sacrificial pioneer work of the Olai Urangs and others bore fruit in the establishment of many new churches in British Columbia, Alberta and Saskatchewan.

During and after World War II, in the 40's, the work of the Association was "looking up" on all fronts. The home mission work was organized on a more substantial basis and a Director of Home Missions engaged. Several Bible conference grounds were acquired. The Association affiliated with the National Association of Evangelicals in 1942. The publication department took a forward step in the purchase of its own press in the spring of 1942. Discussions with the leaders of the Evangelical Free Church of America (the kindred Swedish group) led to the merger of the Minneapolis and the Chicago schools and to the uniting of the publications of the two denominations. This, of course, meant the eventual merger of the denominations as such, which took place in June of 1950, providing a new impetus to the work and the ushering in of a new era in the work of the Evangelical Free Church.

PART III. THE ORIGIN AND DEVELOPMENT OF THE EVANGELICAL FREE CHURCH OF AMERICA

The Swedish Evangelical Free Church owed its existence, in large measure, to a Swedish religious newspaper, *Chicago-Bladet,* established in 1877 by John Martenson, an enterprising and gifted young man who had been deeply influenced by the revivals and the "free church movement" in Sweden. This paper became the voice and champion and unofficial organ of those who eventually associated themselves in the work of the Swedish Evangelical Free Church.

The prophetic Bible conferences sponsored by the newspaper brought together those who became leaders in the new movement, and the detailed reports of these conferences by the editor prepared the way for the conference in Boone, Iowa, in 1884, when the initial steps were taken to form an association, or fellowship of churches, which evolved into the Swedish Evangelical Free Church of America.

The leading personality, in addition to the editor of the paper, in the formation of the association, was a brilliant young theologian, Professor John G. Princell, a former Lutheran clergyman who had been excommunicated from the Augustana Lutheran Synod because of his refusal to administer the Lord's Supper to unbelievers and to admit them to membership in his church. Leaving the presidency of Ansgar College of Knoxville, Ill., he became associate editor of *Chicago-Bladet* from 1880 to 1884, during which time he guided the constituency of *Chicago-Bladet* in the formation of the association, in Boone, in 1884.

Three Decades of Growth (1884-1914)

The first thirty years of the Swedish Evangelical Free Church were years of struggle to come of age. The 21 ministers who comprised the 1884 conference in Boone could count on 27 churches to support the decisions they made. Most of these churches did not have resident pastors but were served by itinerant evangelists.

Growth of the movement was rapid as revival fires were ignited by the "free" preachers who visited the various Swedish communities.

Spiritually this period was characterized by "seasons of refreshing from the presence of the Lord." Doctrinally there were wide differences of opinion and a great variety of emphases, often resulting in considerable debate. Organizationally the local churches were brought closer and closer together in cooperation. Educationally there was considerable progress through the establishment of a Bible Institute for the training of ministers. Evangelistically there was an enlarged vision in the promotion of both home and foreign missions.

The Bible Institute, established in 1897, grew from brief Bible courses of two to three weeks' duration. The courses offered in 1897 and 1898 covered only ten-week periods, but by 1901, largely through the efforts of the Rev. P. J. Elmquist, superintendent of missions, a three-year program was launched, with Professor John G. Princell as the leading personality and teacher.

The home and foreign missionary projects undertaken during this period furthered the spirit of cooperation and unity on the part of the churches. A home mission work was started in Utah to take the Gospel to the Swedes who were being influenced by Mormonism. Nine District societies were organized—in Colorado, Illinois, Wisconsin, Minnesota, Nebraska, Iowa, Texas, California, and South Dakota.

As early as 1887, three years after the beginning of the united work, a mission was commenced in South China, when Hans J. von Qualen, a young Dane educated at the Chicago Theological Seminary, was sent to Canton to carry on an aggressive missionary work. By 1905 the mission consisted of five missionaries and sixteen native helpers.

The urgent need of a residence for the missionaries in China inspired the women in the Chicago churches, who, in 1908, organized the Women's Missionary Society and decided to raise money to build a mission home in Canton. For many years Mrs. Josephine Princell, wife of the distinguished professor, was president of the Society.

Young people's and Sunday school work was promoted through state young people's and Sunday school conferences, there being no national young people's fellowship until 1941.

Benevolent institutions were also established during this period, namely, the Christian Orphans Home of Holdrege, Nebraska, and the Swedish Old People's Home of Boone, Iowa.

While *Chicago-Bladet* continued to serve the churches as an unofficial organ, it was recognized that this paper was a privately owned periodical and could not be depended on always to represent all phases of the Free Church work. Hence an official publication, *Missionstidningen* (The Mission Journal) was established by conference decision in 1913, with the Rev. J. C. Olson as editor.

Commemorating the 30th anniversary of the founding of the Swedish Evangelical Free Church, the executive committee of the denomination published a volume of nearly 400 pages which contained a history of the work from the beginning, including minutes of the annual conferences; a section honoring the pioneer leaders of the work; a summary of the organization and work of the District societies; a listing of the churches in the denomination, with a picture of each; and pictures of most of the ministers in the organization.

The book, printed in Swedish, is entitled *Frikyrkans Minnesskrift* (The Free Church's Book of Remembrance), published in 1914.

By the end of this first 30-year period the Ministerial Association, which had been formed in 1894, had 113 names on its membership roll, and 137 churches considered themselves a part of the Evangelical Free Church fellowship.

Attaining Maturity (1914-1934)

The 20-year period from 1914 to 1934 did not provide the kind of environment nor conditions that were conducive to growth of a fellowship like that of the Swedish Evangelical Free Church. The work was in a period of transition from that of a foreign-language group to that of an English-speaking denomination. Swedish was used almost exclusively up to the time of World War I, but twenty years later when the Golden Jubilee conference was held in Boone, Iowa, English was used almost without exception. The World War had hastened the process of change and in other ways had adversely affected the growth of the denomination.

The end of this period was in the middle of the world-wide Depression, which also had its effect on the spirit and activity of churches and denominations in general.

The annual conferences of the Free Church increased in size considerably during this period, which indicated, if nothing more, that the churches felt their need of each other more than ever. Though there were not many new churches added to the fellowship, the churches that cooperated in the work were more ready to send delegates and participate in the affairs of the united work.

The 1914 conference had only 84 members qualified to vote, whereas, in 1934, at the Golden Jubilee conference, there were 227 delegates and ministers taking part.

Total membership at the beginning of this 20-year period was approximately 5,500. Sunday school enrollment of the churches that reported was 8,719, with 850 teachers and officers. Twenty years later, total membership in the 107 churches whose historical sketches appear in the *Golden Jubilee Book* was 8,139.

This indicates that there was no increase in the *number* of churches, but also that there was a substantial increase in the *strength* of the cooperating churches.

Progress during this period is evident in the expansion of the foreign mission work from one field to four; in the re-establishment of a Bible Institute, with a high school department, operating in its own building; in the acquisition of *Chicago-Bladet* as an official paper, and the launching of an all-English periodical, *The Evangelical Beacon;* in the establishment of a headquarters office with a full-time president and staff, and in the realization that the fellowship was no longer a foreign-language group serving a limited constituency but one of the agencies God wanted to use to make a spiritual impact upon people of *all* backgrounds and nationalities.

The foreign mission expansion included the taking over of a mission field in North China, the opening of work in Venezuela, the launching of a new work in the Belgian Congo, and the strengthening of the work in South China.

With the purchase of the newspaper *Chicago-Bladet* in 1926 and the launching of an all-English periodical, *The Evangelical Beacon,* in 1931, recognition was given to the importance of the printed page in the promotion of the Lord's work.

The passing of Professor John G. Princell, in 1915, created a crisis in the Bible Institute program. An effort to secure Professor A. L. Wedell of Minnehaha Academy, in Minneapolis, to succeed him was unsuccessful. It seemed expedient to seek an affiliation with the Moody Bible Institute, which was willing to provide classroom space and other facilities on condition that the Free Church remunerate its own instructors in this so-called "Swedish department" of Moody. An instructor and leader was available in the person of the Rev. Gustav Edwards, a former missionary from China who had been home a few years studying at Chicago Theological Seminary and Wheaton College. The school opened in the fall of 1916 with one teacher and one student! At the end of the second year Dr. Edwards reported that 30 students had received instruction during the year and that an additional teacher had beeen engaged on a part-time basis, namely, Miss Anna J. Lindgren, a former school teacher from Sweden who was studying at the Moody Bible Institute.

The school at Moody grew so that at times there were as many as a hundred students enrolled. However, there was recognition of the need of a high school department, since most of the young men and women enrolling in the Bible Institute were not high school graduates. On recommendation of the school board, in 1923, Professor A. L. Wedell, at that time principal of a high school in Hilmar, Calif., was engaged as an instructor, with the expectation that he would inaugurate a high school department. An old mansion at 4211 N. Hermitage Ave., Chicago, was purchased in 1925 and was ready for occupancy in January of 1926 by both the Bible Institute and the newly organized academy, or high school department. Within a very few years the academy was accredited by the University of Illinois.

During this brief 20-year period the Women's Missionary Society won more and more recognition as a strong arm of the united Free Church work. After completing its first project—the mission home in Canton—they took on one project after another and always went "over the top" in raising the money to complete their project.

The home mission work during this period received its principal emphasis and development through the strengthening of the various District organizations. While the foreign mission work had its well-organized Board of Foreign Missions, no such board for general home mission extension existed, though at the 1934 conference a "Commission on Evangelism and Extension" was elected.

The financial strength of the Evangelical Free Church gained considerably during this period. Properties belonging to the denomination in 1920 were valued at $113,500. Seven years later, total assets were more than half a million dollars.

The difficult period of transition from a foreign-language church serving a Scandinavian constituency to an all-English denomination with a world-wide vision came to an end with the observance of the 50th anniversary of the Free Church in 1934. By this time our leaders realized that the future growth of the work depended upon the extent to which they recognized that their field was no longer limited to people of one nationality or language. Having caught a vision of an Evangelical Free Church without national or language barriers, the Free Church people were prepared for the kind of advance they had not seen since the revival days at the beginning of the Free Church movement.

Renewed Vitality (1934-1950)

The story of the last 15-year period of the Evangelical Free Church of America up to the time of the merger with the Evangelical Free Church Association (formerly the Norwegian-Danish Evangelical Free Church Association) demonstrates not only that the Evangelical Free Church was determined to live, in spite of the new conditions, but that it had caught a vision of future possibilities it had never had before.

Financial reports at the annual conferences tell part of the story. Receipts reported by the financial secretary increased from $40,000 to $262,000 between 1935 and 1949.

Total membership of the churches increased from 8,139 in 1934 to 13,500 by 1949. Sunday school enrollment increased from 9,100 in 1938 to 22,500 in 1949. The number of churches increased from 132 in 1938 to 193 by 1949.

A stronger emphasis on home missions provided much of the impetus for expansion of the work on the home front, especially with the coming of the Rev. A. J. Thorwall as field secretary and director of evangelism. An official home mission board finally materialized in 1947.

The foreign work did not suffer by the new emphasis on home missions. In 1935 there were ten missionaries in the Congo, seven in Venezuela, and four in Canton, actually on the field. By 1941 the foregin missionary corps had risen to 33 on three fields—11 in Congo, nine in China and Hong Kong, and 13 in Venezuela.

The largest of our mission stations in the Congo was turned over to the Mission Covenant Church in 1937. In spite of this, however, the Free Church, in the spring of 1950, still had four main stations, with 12 missionaries on the field, three main station churches, 17 district churches, 133 village chapels, 4,050 church members, 2,748 candidates for baptism, three main station schools with 21 native teachers and 430 pupils enrolled; also 105 village day schools with 2,634 pupils, and a medical work that provided 21,234 general examinations and 18,755 general treatments during the year.

New enthusiasm was engendered by the opening of a new mission field in Japan in 1948 and 1949, with the Rev. and Mrs. Calvin Hanson as the pioneers in this field.

The rapid growth of the high school department of our school was hindering the development of the Bible Institute, located in the same building. The 1938 conference voted to discontinue the academy to accelerate the growth of the Bible Institute and Seminary.

Not only did the Bible Institute receive a new surge of life, with the elimination of the high school department, but, under the direction of President A. L. Wedell, a three-year Seminary course was inaugurated. Enrollment by 1940 had increased to 81, including 24 young men in the Seminary. Even without the academy, it was becoming evident that better and larger quarters were needed for the development of the school. Giving his last report to the conference (before his death in 1940), Professor Wedell said, "I am not convinced that the Free Church people are willing and able to make the sacrifices necessary for a new building, but that it *can* be done and *should* be done is quite evident."

Our school operated on an extremely small budget during the early 40's. Part-time instructors were used as much as possible. The record shows that total salaries paid to faculty and staff in 1944 aggregated only $9,369.00!

A successful campaign to raise money for a new school building was launched in 1943 and the goal of $95,000 was in sight within one year. Construction was delayed, however, because of the war and because the building committee had its eyes on a campus in one of the Chicago suburbs that was expected to be for sale. Another reason for the delay was the interest shown by some of the leaders of the Evangelical Free Church Association in a possible merger of their school with the Chicago school.

Thus the golden anniversary of the school (in 1947), in a sense marked the end of its existence as a separate institution. A new era was about to be ushered in for our school work as well as for our Free Church work as a whole.

The 1946 conferences of the two Free Church bodies had approved the "idea of merger" so far as the schools were concerned and negotiations between the authorized committees of the two groups began without further delay. After considerable discussion, it was decided to locate the united school on the campus of the Chicago school. Dedication of the new building, at the corner of North Hermitage and Berteau avenues, took place on May 28, 1950, a few weeks before the consummation of the merger of the two denominations.

In the meantime the publications of the two groups had been merged, the Chicago office moving to Minneapolis. The small print shop that had been operated by the Free Church Association became a joint project. *The Evangelist* and *The Evangelical Beacon* became *The Evangelical Beacon and Evangelist.*

Before the actual completion of the merger of the two groups, the Evangelical Free Church of America purchased a building at 2950 Nicollet Ave., Minneapolis, where it was possible to open a much larger and more attractive book store, print shop and publication office, as well as a national headquarters for the denomination. The Free Church took possession of the building in April of 1950, just two months prior to the historic merger conference in June of 1950.

The Women's Missionary Society of the Evangelical Free Church celebrated its 40th anniversary in 1948, at which time it was reported that at least $170,000 had been raised by the women during the 40-year period, during which they had taken on and completed a large number of home and foreign missionary projects.

The young people's work of the Evangelical Free Church received a powerful new impetus with the formation of a national youth organization in 1941. The Free Church Youth Fellowship took on several very ambitious projects during the first years of its existence, publishing a paper, supporting missionaries, etc. They were still going strong when they set their budget of $25,000 for the 1949-50 year and called a director for the coming year. Like other branches of the work, however, the FCYF was to enter a new stage of development through the merger of the two denominations.

The Ministerial Association commemorated its 50th anniversary in 1945 (a year late) by publishing a book containing a picture and a brief meditation by each of its members. Membership exceeded 200 at that time, and increased to 280 by 1949, the year before the merger.

As early as 1945 a national Sunday school committee was elected, which recommended that a full-time, or at least a part-time, director of Christian Education be engaged by the Evangelical Free Church. The pending merger of the two groups necessitated the postponement of this action until such time as the merger should be consummated.

During World War II an active Servicemen's department was conducted, which ministered to the Free Church servicemen in many ways. Mel Larson, associate editor of *The Evangelical Beacon,* headed this department, which included a special Servicemen's Page in the *Beacon.*

Just six years before the merger (in 1944) a workable plan was finally adopted which would provide a small pension for retired ministers. By 1950 membership in the Ministers Annuity and Aid Plan included 180 persons, including 22 women missionaries.

PART IV. THE STORY OF THE MERGER

The merger of the Evangelical Free Church Association and the Evangelical Free Church of America, in June of 1950, was the culmination of a long series of efforts to accomplish this end by leaders in both groups. On several occasions committees had been appointed to consider such a merger. A definite plan was outlined in 1938 and submitted to the two groups, but the results of the referendum indicated that the time was not yet ripe for merger.

Dr. Olson listed the "road-blocks" to merger at that time as (1) the difference in language, (2) the nationalistic spirit that still prevailed, and (3) fear of too strong an organization.

While officially the merger question was dropped in 1940, leaders of both groups continued to get together to discuss the subject in an unofficial manner. The idea occurred to some that the place to begin was the uniting of the publications and schools. They knew that the complete merger of the two bodies would then follow naturally and with very little opposition.

Both of the Free Church conferences approved the merger of the schools and publications in 1946. Operation of the two schools under a united Board of Education began in the fall of the same year, and in July of 1947 the publications of the two groups began to operate, in Minneapolis.

A "Resolution of Merger" drawn up by Dr. Arnold Olson was adopted by both conferences in 1948, which carried without a dissenting vote in the conference of The Evangelical Free Church of America and with very little opposition in the conference of the Free Church Association.

Dr. Olson became the logical chairman of the Merger Committee, which ironed out all the anticipated problems of the merger so that when the final plan was submitted to the respective conferences, the vote in favor of the merger was practically unanimous. In the referendum submitted to the churches only two out of the 207 churches that responded by the time of the deadline indicated their disapproval. These two churches, however, changed their vote to favor the plan before the conference date was reached.

The merger conference, June 13-18, 1950, at Medicine Lake, near Minneapolis, was an unforgettable event. After the two groups had conducted their own final conferences, the two groups assembled in joint conference and formed the new organization.

Any sadness that might have been felt as "finis" was being written over the history of the two organizations was soon dissipated in the thought that the new organization was to inherit all the spiritual resources of both of these mature organizations that were now passing off the scene.

The inspirational rally following the transaction of this important business was a spiritual experience for the huge crowd that filled the mammoth auditorium. Participating were Dr. Arnold Olson, chairman of the Merger Committee; Dr. E. A. Halleen, who for 28 years had been president of the larger of the two groups; Pastor Joseph Swan, who had been president of the Association, and Mr. John S. Nyquist, Sr., legal member of the Merger Committee.

One of the last items of business on the agenda for the united conference was the turning over of the key to the new administration building to the united Board of Trustees. Thus the usually vexing "housing problem" had already been solved for the two parties that had entered into the "marriage contract."

The editor of *The Evangelical Beacon,* commenting on the merger, wrote, "The new organization will now reap the benefits of the best that has been achieved by both groups through the use of the best gifts and facilities that have been found in the respective groups of the past."

The dramatic story of what happened in the first nine years following the merger, told by Mel Larson in the concluding chapter of the *Diamond Jubilee Story,* is a striking illustration of the strengthened testimony that was established through the uniting of the two Evangelical Free Church groups.

PART V. NINE YEARS OF MERGER

1950-1951. The first annual conference of the united Evangelical Free Church brought 1,000 delegates to the general sessions, Women's Missionary Society, Ministerial Association, and Free Church Youth Fellowship to Winona Lake, Indiana. The conference was characterized by a remarkable spirit of unity, with no sign of schism in the newly created body. It was evident that they were no longer two separate groups trying to work together for harmony. The two were one in such a real way that there was little awareness of the former division.

Dr. E. A. Halleen, elected president of the united Free Church at the merger conference, served in this capacity for the last time and was voted president emeritus for the remainder of his life. Dr. Arnold Olson became president-elect.

Dr. Halleen reported on progress during this first year of merger: Overseas, the work in the Philippines had been started. Rev. H. G. Rodine had been engaged as secretary of foreign missions.

Trinity reported an enrollment of 163, with 99 men and 64 women. High spot of the school year was the inauguration of

Dr. C. Raymond Ludwigson as president, on Thursday night of the conference.

All other departments and organizations had experienced the same mushrooming impact of the merger. *The Evangelical Beacon and Evangelist* reported a circulation of 8,700 copies, with 64 churches on the church-sponsored subscription plan. The Women's Missionary Society had completed its $21,000 drive to furnish the new dormitories at Trinity. More than $20,000 had been raised by FCYF'ers for their many projects at home and abroad.

From all sides came the wonderful reaction, "The merger is working! The merger is working!" It was evident that the merger not only had been *of* God, but that it was being blessed *by* God. Everyone seemed more willing to heed the conference theme, "Occupy Till I Come," as they headed home from the conference.

1951-1952. Early in January the Department of Evangelism added the Rev. C. Chester Larson to its staff, with an emphasis on children's meetings.

There was rejoicing in the news that Dr. Titus Johnson, founder of the Free Church work in Congo, had agreed to return to the field to assist in establishing a hospital.

Back at Winona Lake again, in June, the reports of progress were most encouraging. Twenty-three churches had been started or had affiliated during the year—one every 16 days. Approval was given to the first million dollar budget. Circulation of *The Evangelical Beacon and Evangelist* was up to 9,000. The Swedish-language paper, *Chicago-Bladet,* had been discontinued, closing its more than 75 years of ministry.

This was the final conference in which Dr. Halleen served as president. A kind of "swan song" in his report pronounced a benediction on the pastors, as he said,

> May God's choice blessing rest upon our pastors as well as upon the churches and the manifold activities. My sincere prayer is that Christ, our great Commander, may lead our dear

Free Church to greater victories. May we all be found watching and waiting when He comes for His own!

On Friday night of the conference Arnold Theodore Olson was installed as the new president. There was no question but that he was God's appointed leader for the united group. Born in Minneapolis and reared in the Evangelical Free Church, a graduate of Trinity of Minneapolis, with 22 years of experience as a pastor, in addition to his experience as a World War II chaplain, he was eminently qualified to assume the leadership of the united Evangelical Free Church of America.

1952-1953. The new president of the Evangelical Free Church opened his heart to his people. "I do not intend," he declared, "to try to fill the shoes of my illustrious predecessor. I shall, on the other hand, endeavor to do my very best to the limits of my ability through the enabling power of the Chief Shepherd."

The annual conference, at Winona Lake, was the largest to date, with 455 voting delegates and an estimated 3,000 people present during the week.

The Home Mission department reported that 24 new churches had been added to the Free Church fellowship—one for every 15 and one-half days. Our evangelists reported some 1,200 decisions for Christ. The Sunday school committee was elevated to board status and the FCYF was tied in more closely through its executive secretary operating from headquarters.

Highlight of the meeting was the significant accomplishment of the Women's Missionary Society in completing in one year its two-year goal of $27,000 for the new hospital in the Congo.

Dr. Olson's comment following his first year in office was significant. "I am convinced," he said, "that the future opportunities for the Evangelical Free Church of America surpass anything we have experienced in the past. Our only limitations will come through lack of vision and faith." He also stresssed "the need of positive Gospel preaching in our pulpits, prevailing prayer in the pews, and a new passion and purity in the lives of our people."

1953-1954. Personnel changes brought the Rev. C. Chester Larson to headquarters as acting secretary of the new Sunday School department, and took Mel Larson from our promotion and servicemen's departments to Wheaton to become editor of the *Youth for Christ Magazine.*

Mount Hermon, Calif. was the site of the 70th annual conference. A greeting to the conference from President Dwight Eisenhower extended congratulations. He expressed interest in the ties that Mrs. Eisenhower's family had with the Evangelical Free Church. (Mrs. Eisenhower's grandparents were members of the host church in Boone, Iowa, when the first conference was held there in 1884. Her uncle was treasurer of our Evangelical Free Church Home for many years and her aunt was organist at our Boone church for a generation).

A major decision of the conference involved the changing of the children's home at Holdrege, Nebraska, into a home for the aged.

The addition of twenty new churches during the year had brought the total number of churches in the Evangelical Free Church of America to 351. Sixty-four new church buildings were completed in the 12-month period.

Enrollment at Trinity had reached 229, with a goal of 338 set for 1958. The school had said farewell to Miss Hilda Carlson after 29 years of devoted service as cook, matron, and dean of women. Circulation of the *Beacon* had passed the 10,000 figure.

Nine words from the Word of God as repeated by President Olson rang in the ears of more than one delegate as they headed home from the conference: "There remaineth yet very much land to be possessed."

1954-1955. Important events of this year provided major news in the spring of 1955. One was the ground-breaking for the Bible Institute at El Limon, Venezuela. The other was the dedication of the hospital at Tandala, in the Congo. Six thousand people gathered on this memorable May 17, 1955. Dr. Olson and Mr. G. W. Aldeen were the official representatives of the EFCA at the dedication. The 30-acre plot has 11 permanent buildings on it. Plans were drawn by Dr. Titus Johnson. The prayers of many Free Church people over a period of many years were answered in the completion and dedication of this greatly needed hospital facility.

At the 1955 conference a seven-man committee brought to the conference a Program of Progress for the Diamond Jubilee of the Evangelical Free Church of America—a program to be achieved in the years prior to June, 1959.

The conference had 457 voting delegates, with 1,014 registered for the main and affiliate conferences. It was reported that 16 new churches had been added to the fellowship, with ten others in the formative stages.

With 18 new missionaries, the roster now totaled 130 serving under our Board of Foreign Missions.

Major changes found Dr. C. Raymond Ludwigson leaving Trinity and returning to Wheaton, and Milford Sholund, Dean at Trinity, going to Gospel Light Press as director of research. Other departments had encouraging reports, with circulation of the *Beacon* up to 11,000 and with substantial net profits reported by the Beacon Book Store and the Free Church Press.

This was the farewell conference for the Rev. A. J. Thorwall, "everybody's friend," the director of evangelism. His report, on the occasion of his retirement, stressed the importance of a passion for evangelism. "When a church ceases to evangelize, she ceases to be evangelical. When she ceases to glow, she ceases to grow."

Dr. Olson had traveled 124,000 miles in the previous twelve months. He set the tone of the conference when he said in his annual report,

> The theme has been well chosen, "The Hope Set Before Us."
> It places emphasis on the future and does so with optimism . . .
> A spirit of pessimism and cynicism has taken the place of faith

and hope . . . Having found these man-made candles going out one by one, men are now ready to seek the deeper things of life. Spiritual bankruptcy is the first step to obtaining a spiritual inheritance . . . This is an hour of the Church's greatest challenge. If we fail, we may have had our last opportunity.

1955-1956. Highlights of the year included the appointment of Dr. T. B. Madsen as acting president of Trinity, and the dedication of the new Christian Homes, Inc., for the aged, in Holdrege, Nebraska. Death took two prominent Free Church women, namely, Mrs. A. J. Thorwall and Mrs. Victor Carlson, the latter a former president of the national W.M.S.; and one of the leading laymen of the EFCA, Mr. J. Richard Johnson of Rockford.

Florida was opened up for Free Church work as the Rev. Herbert Kyrk went to Lakeland and the Rev. Fred Haas pioneered in North Miami Beach. Dr. Olson commented on this new advance, "With the two new congregations in Florida, it can now be said that the influence of the Free Church stretches from coast to coast, from Maine to Florida, and from Washington to California, and more than half way across the Dominion of Canada."

Thirty-eight new churches were welcomed into the EFCA, including 15 in Canada through affiliation.

Of interest was the report that 216 missionaries now were serving under either our Free Church board or that of the Evangelical Alliance Mission, or one missionary for every 120 members. First steps were taken to begin work in Singapore in commissioning the Rev. Arthur G. Lindquist of Hong Kong to survey the field.

The Program of Progress goal was raised from $300,000 to $800,000, with fifty percent to remain in the local churches. Other goals set for the Diamond Jubilee Year were:

        75 new churches
        75 new Sunday schools
        75 new FCYF groups
        75 new WMS groups

7500 new members
  75 new missionaries
  75 new seminary students at Trinity
7500 new subscribers to the *Beacon.*

1956-1957. Two silver anniversaries were observed in the fall of 1956. *The Evangelical Beacon* marked the 25th anniversary of its ministry by a special issue on September 18. The Evangelical Mountain Mission, in Kentucky, observed its 25th anniversary November 1-4.

The year 1957 had been designated the Jubilee Year of Evangelism. Many signed pledges in January vowing to put God first in personal disciplines, public privileges, and the program of outreach. Through many channels a special soul-winning emphasis was carried on in our churches throughout the year.

The work in Canada was strengthened through the affiliation of 18 more churches, formerly associated with the Fellowship of Gospel Churches.

Dr. H. Wilbert Norton was nominated by the Board of Education as the new president of Trinity and installed on Thursday night of the conference. Dr. G. Douglas Young was named dean of the seminary and Gunnar Urang dean of the college.

The 1957 conference, held at Ocean Grove, New Jersey, had 1,065 registered visitors and delegates, including 392 voting members.

A gain of 22 new churches was reported for the year. Total membership now stood at 27,203. Dr. Olson was elected to a third three-year term and layman Paul Carlson was re-elected moderator.

As the Women's Missionary Society elected a new slate of officers, a "Nebraska slate," with Mrs. Willard J. Eckman as president, the Iowa board, guided by Mrs. D. L. Foster, looked back over the past six years during which time projects totaling $122,457.23 had been completed.

1957-1958. New work in Singapore and Malaysia was started —the sixth field to be entered by the Evangelical Free Church.

The inauguration of Dr. Norton as president of Trinity took place on November 21, 1957, at the First Evangelical Free Church (Summerdale) of Chicago, Dr. Norton's home church.

The first 11 churches holding Jubilee banquets for the Program of Progress pledged $196,000—an indication that the goal of $800,000 (raised from $300,000 two years previously) was far too low. As conference time approached, it was reported that this figure had been raised to $832,888.30, with only 35 churches so far having participated. It was evident that even the $800,000 goal was much too low, whereupon, on recommendation of the Board of Directors, the goal was raised to $2,500,000, with half of the amounts raised to remain with the local churches.

Some of the other goals had also been too low! The goal of 75 new churches had been too low; 93 new churches had been added since the goal was established, and instead of 75 new Seminary students for Trinity, there were 136. The goal of 12,000 new Sunday school members had also been too low, with more than 13,000 reported.

The news of former President E. A. Halleen's home-going, at the age of 83, saddened our constituency. Memorial services were held at the Central Free Church of Minneapolis, where he was a member, on January 18, 1958. The Rev. Carroll Nelson, who had been Dr. Halleen's pastor at Central for several years, gave this striking tribute to him:

> God gave a wonderful gift to the Evangelical Free Church when He gave us Dr. E. A. Halleen. Staunch in spiritual and moral principles, sterling in character, striking in appearance, strong in the pulpit, apparently always serene and stable, our brother has walked among us displaying so many of those excellent graces men wish for and often lack. His influence for Christ has been in evidence throughout our Evangelical Free Church from center to circumference.

Total membership in the EFCA churches at conference time was almost 30,000, an increase of 2,450 over the preceding year. Twenty-nine new churches had been added, bringing the total to 419. Enrollment at Trinity had reached an all-time high with 317 students. The EFCA ranked third again in per capita giving. A significant advance was the setting up of the Christian Investors Foundation, a place for Free Church people to invest their money and allow it to work in assisting churches with their building programs with low-interest loans.

1958-1959. The Jubilee Fund continued to grow during the summer and fall of 1958, and by the end of the year stood at $1,422,806.34 as church after church participated with enthusiasm.

The Evangelical Beacon, with its new editor at the helm, Mr. Mel Larson, was making its influence felt in all phases of our Free Church work. The former editor began serving in his new capacity as secretary of publications, with special emphasis on the publishing of books.

Looking forward to the Diamond Jubilee Conference, Dr. Olson commented, in the last issue of *The Evangelical Beacon* in 1958:

There will be a great deal of reminiscing during the coming year. Triumphs and tragedies will be reviewed. Experiences of the past, sad and hilarious, will be reported. The pioneers of the early years will be honored.

But we are not on a pilgrimage to the shrines of yesterday. We are in a crusade to plant flags in new territories for Christ. We have not yet caught up with our horizons. Those who met for the first conference in 1884 never dreamed that the work would be as far-reaching as it is today. In fact, they didn't even expect the Church of Christ to be on earth this long.

Let us not wait until the 75th annual conference to move forward. Let us begin with a time of re-dedication during Prayer Week. We need not pray for the Lord's presence. We need but pray for courage and for faith, for eyes to see the vision and ears to hear the call. This is the Year of Jubilee. It is also a year of decision.

The following facts and figures are appended to Mel Larson's story of Nine Years of Merger, up-to-date as of January 1, 1959, at the beginning of the Diamond Jubilee Year:

We have 443 local congregations or Sunday schools with a total membership of approximately 31,915. A total of 173 new churches were started or affiliated or an average of 20 a year in the eight years and six months since the merger.

The Ministerial Association has 576 members in good standing. Trinity Seminary and Bible College has 293 students enrolled. The faculty and staff number 35.

The Sunday schools have a total enrollment of more than 60,000.

Three homes are operated for our senior citizens: one at Boone, Iowa, one at Holdrege, Nebraska, and one at Princeton, Minn.

Two homes for children are operated: the Christian Home for Children at Fort Lee, New Jersey, and the Lydia Children's Home of Chicago.

The Beacon Book Store, in Minneapolis, has five fulltime employees and grosses about $160,000 yearly. Free Church Press has 15 full-time workers and grosses nearly $200,000 yearly. Circulation of *The Evangelical Beacon* is at 13,700 copies.

Overseas, our missionary roster numbers 147 on seven fields.

In addition, 91 missionaries from local Evangelical Free churches are serving under the Evangelical Alliance Mission (TEAM).

Concluding his section of the book, Mel Larson writes:

This, then, is the human report on the first 75 years of the Evangelical Free Church of America. We trust it will not differ too greatly from the record God has kept.

The future? It rests with God. That is all we need to know.

TWO

JUBILEE YEAR

THE DIAMOND JUBILEE YEAR

T HE JUBILEE YEAR IS HERE!" This was uppermost in the mind of the editor of *The Evangelical Beacon* as he made ready the first issue of the denominational magazine in 1959. "We rejoice," he wrote, "that our 75th anniversary year of the Evangelical Free Church of America has arrived!" He then reminded us that anniversaries of this kind not only provide opportunity for a survey of the past, but stimulate our efforts in the light of the challenge they offer. "Let us rejoice," he reflects, in what God has accomplished throughout the past seventy-five years, but "let us also roll up our sleeves a bit more and become increasingly more active in presenting Christ to this our generation."

Careful preparations had been made ahead of time for the observance of this anniversary. Dr. Arnold Olson, president of the Evangelical Free Church of America, in his annual report to the 71st general conference, in 1955, reminded us that the Diamond Jubilee was only four years away. "We must make plans for this great event," he wrote, and then announced that some plans had already been made. An editorial board had been set up for the preparation of a history of the 75-year period. A commission had been appointed to prepare a program for advance covering of the four-year period leading up to the Diamond Jubilee. The group had already been at work and were coming to the conference with specific proposals for a program of progress. Their program was designed to (1) deepen the spiritual life of our constituency, (2) to develop and extend all the tangible facilities to increase our effectiveness in spreading the Gospel so that there might be (3) a great impact for Christ on our community, nation and world.

With these objectives in mind a program was outlined with (1) the emphasis on Christian Education in 1956, (2) on Soul-winning and Evangelism in 1957, (3) a concentration on Missions in 1958 and (4) an emphasis on Extension in 1959.

When final approval was given by the conference to this program, the financial goal had been raised from $300,000 to $800,000, with half of the proceeds designated for the above-mentioned project plus $100,000 for the Revolving Fund, with which to assist local churches in financing their building projects.

From the very beginning of the Jubilee Year there was considerable excitement and keen anticipation as Free Church people looked forward to the Diamond Jubilee conference in June. Denver, Colorado, had been chosen as the location for the conference, partly because the First Evangelical Free Church of this city was one of the oldest churches in our fellowship and one of the original 27 churches to form the association of churches in Boone in 1884. The facilities of the Colorado Women's College had been engaged for the conference. Buildings on the campus were announced as Halleen Hall, Dyrness Hall, Eielson and Tweed Halls, and Princell and L. J. Pedersen dormitories, thus honoring the memory of Free Church pioneer leaders in our work.

The theme chosen for the conference was "Forward in the Faith of Our Fathers." The messages, delivered at the conference, have been preserved in a paper-back volume published some weeks after the conference. Included are Dr. Arnold Olson's sermon on the general theme, followed by messages from Free Church leaders on such subjects as "Forward in the Work of Our Fathers," "Forward in the Vision of Our Fathers," "Forward in the Hope of Our Fathers," etc.

The Diamond Jubilee conference was the largest in the history of general conferences, with 760 voting members.

Important decisions of the conference included the election of the Rev. Herbert Kyrk as secretary of home missions and the Rev. C. Chester Larson as secretary of Sunday school work.

The conference also authorized the Board of Education to purchase property "either adjacent to or not adjacent to the present school property" for the development of our school program on an adequate campus. Enlargement of the board was also authorized.

The board was also authorized to make plans for the establishment of a junior college in British Columbia, in response to a presentation of the need of such a school by leaders in our Canadian churches.

Enthusiasm ran high as reports were given by leaders of our work. The goal of 75 new congregations by 1959, set four years previously, had been entirely too conservative, since 128 congregations had been started or affiliated during this period. More than 10,000 new members had been added to membership rolls instead of 7,500. Eighty-four new missionaries (including 24 under TEAM) had been added to missionary personnel instead of 75. No less than 123 students had enrolled in our seminary instead of 75, and 13,565 new pupils had been enrolled in our Sunday schools instead of 7,500. The goal of 7,500 new subscribers to the *Beacon* had not been reached, but there had been a great surge of new interest in the magazine under the enthusiastic and capable editorship of Mel Larson, whose circulation goals have always been set higher than might seem attainable.

The president's annual report to the conference was most illum-

inating, thought-provoking and challenging. Based on Proverbs
13:22, "A good man leaveth an inheritance to his children's children," he reported that (1) *We have added to our inheritance* as
we have grown in membership (from 27 churches to 452 since
1884) and matured in stewardship (with per capita giving the
highest on record), and enlarged our borders (reaching new areas
of our country), and broadened our fellowship (cooperating with
the International Federation of Free Evangelical Churches). (2)
We have also maintained our inheritance by learning to know the
nature and extent of that inheritance (publishing books of information and instruction); by teaching our children (in Sunday school
work); by training future leaders (in our college and seminary),
and by setting aside men and women for the work of the ministry
(licensing and ordaining men for this purpose).

His report also asked several very searching questions as to
whether or not we might have lost a portion of our inheritance
since it was turned over to us by the pioneer founders of our work.
"Have we lost that sense of personal responsibility so willingly
accepted by our fathers? Have we lost the fervor of our fathers?
And have we lost the vision of our fathers?"

The presentation of the *Diamond Jubilee Story* was a highlight
of the conference, according to Editor Mel Larson, from whom
we quote:

> The platform of Smiley Junior High was stacked with books,
> as was the foyer where book store manager Stanley Noreen
> sold copies after the meeting. Editor-in-chief Roy A. Thompson
> presented the first copy to President Olson. Dr. Olson, in turn,
> surprised Thompson by giving to him a volume similar to the
> one presented to President and Mrs. Eisenhower and to Con-
> gressman Cederberg. Leather-bound volumes were then pre-
> sented to co-authors Dr. H. W. Norton, Rev. Olai Urang and
> Mel Larson, and the names of the sponsors (those who had
> helped to finance the project), were read by Thompson. These,
> too, received leather-bound copies . . . It was a memorable
> moment.

The June 30 issue of *The Evangelical Beacon* carried a cover picture of Dr. Arnold Olson and President Dwight Eisenhower, taken at the White House. Free Church Congressman Elford Cederberg, member of our Bay City, Mich. church, had made an appointment at the White House at which time it was the privilege of Dr. Olson to present two beautifully bound copies of the *Diamond Jubilee Story* (in red cowhide) to the president, one for himself and one for his wife, whose grandparents were members of the host church in Boone, Iowa, when the first conference was held there in 1884.

Specific accomplishments reported at our Diamond Jubilee conference included the establishment of the Southeastern District, organized in 1958; the establishment of a new work in the Province of Ontario; the organization of Gospel Films at Headquarters; the opening of two new overseas mission fields, namely in Malaysia and Europe. The Bible Institute buildings at El Limon, Venezuela, were nearing completion. Construction had begun for a new Bible Institute in the Congo, and a building had been purchased for the new Bible Institute in Hong Kong. A new book store had been opened in Caracas and a new book store in Hong Kong with a publishing program. A reading center had been opened in the Philippines and two such centers and literature depots in the Congo.

The Jubilee Program had assisted in the expanding of tangible facilities of our churches. No less than 148 churches reported either construction of new buildings, enlargement of present structures, or the purchase of land for development. Plans were also announced for an expansion program of Trinity Seminary and Bible College.

The success of the Jubilee Fund drive was an indication of the enthusiasm and spirit of cooperation that characterized our churches. Again and again the churches which had completed their Jubilee campaigns testified as to the spiritual results of those campaigns. One congregation, rejoicing in the enlarged vision as a result of the program, voted to include the General Fund of the denomination in its annual budget. One pastor wrote, "Our Program of

Progress giving is not only up-to-date, but it is also ahead of schedule. I am certain that our farming community has learned that 'he that soweth sparingly shall also reap sparingly,' so they have given liberally out of the goodness of their hearts and their love for God."

Another pastor wrote, "The results of the Jubilee campaign in our church overwhelmed us . . . Everyone is amazed at the monthly response . . . Even this, however, fades in the light of the greater spiritual blessings which have resulted. We all saw a new vision of what great things our great God can do."

With that spirit possessing our churches, it isn't any wonder that, as early as June 1 of the Jubilee Year, it could be reported that already 139 churches had covenanted to give $1,965,322.74 to the Jubilee Fund and an additional $65,455 to special home mission projects, or a total of $2,030,777.74. At that time another 100 churches were making plans for their participation in the campaign.

This spirit of giving (with its spiritual results) continued throughout the remainder of the Jubilee Year so that it could be reported at the end of the year that the total had reached $2,255,003. Actual cash received had enabled our Headquarters people to turn over $75,000 to Trinity Seminary and Bible College for debt reduction and another $75,000 transferred to Trinity for expansion purposes. Another $75,000 was transferred to the two missionary funds for capital expansion at home and abroad. "As the funds continue to come in," Dr. Olson wrote in the December 22, 1959 issue of the *Beacon*, "$75,000 will be used to pay off the indebtedness on the headquarters building and set up a reserve fund for anticipated expansion. The next $100,000 will go to the Revolving Fund enabling us to grant loans to more churches and also increase the amount of the loans. From that point on and until the sum of $1,250,000 (half of the goal of $2,500,000) has been reached, the money will be used for expansion at Trinity."

A fitting gesture of appreciation and commendation for superb leadership of our Evangelical Free Church of America was given to President Olson by Trinity Seminary and Bible College at the 62d commencement exercises in June of this Jubilee Year when an honorary Doctor of Divinity degree was conferred upon him. At the same time a Doctor of Letters degree was conferred upon Dr. T. B. Madsen, vice president of Trinity and a teacher at our schools for forty years.

The Ministerial Association of the Evangelical Free Church took a forward step at its annual conference—its 65th—during this Diamond Jubilee Year when it made a unanimous decision to adopt a group hospitalization plan offered by the Ministers Life and Casualty Union, thus assuring the ministers of substantial help in time of illness for their families. Forty new names were added to the membership of the Association, bringing the total to 639, compared with the 37 members who organized the Association in 1894.

Another significant event during this Jubilee Year was the fact that the Christian Investors Foundation, approved at the 1958 conference, was now "open for business." Mr. Paul Carlson, a past moderator of the EFCA conference, who had been appointed as secretary-treasurer of the Foundation, received the first investment money of $10,000 from the Rev. Ivan Larson, superintendent of the Christian Homes, Inc. of Holdrege, Nebraska out of a fund that was being held for future expansion of the Home.

The Women's Missionary Society observed its 51st anniversary during the year and turned over a check for $14,000 to Trinity for furnishing a girls' dormitory for Trinity. Its project for the ensuing year would be the purchase of a missionary furlough home to provide housing for missionaries on furlough.

The Free Church Youth Fellowship moved forward at this year's conference by making plans for engaging a full-time executive secretary to work among the local, regional, state and national FCYF groups.

The big event of the year from the standpoint of our Overseas Missions department was the decision to open a medical facility in Hong Kong. For a long time the need of such a facility had been recognized by our missionaries in Hong Kong, who had made this a special subject of prayer. Now at last, not one but two doctors were available for this project, namely, Dr. Robert Chapman and Dr. Gordon Addington. It was announced that Dr. Chapman would leave for the field in January of 1960 and Dr. Addington would follow in July. The enthusiasm for the project expressed itself in donations of money and equipment that encouraged the doctors who had dedicated their lives to this ministry. The story of the "miracle" that made possible not a mere "clinic" but a modern hospital in Hong Kong will be told in another chapter.

A special anniversary issue of *The Evangelical Beacon*—twice the usual size—was published late in October of the Jubilee Year. In it tribute was paid to four pioneers of our work who were still living, namely, the Rev. Frank W. Anderson, who was pastor of the First Evangelical Free Church of Chicago for 33 years and a leader in all phases of Free Church work; the Rev. Thorvald Johansen of Ridgefield, New Jersey, a former missionary who became superintendent of the Christian Home for Children at Fort Lee, New Jersey, and chairman of the Western Association of the Evangelical Free Church Association and secretary of the Eastern Association; the Rev. Ingvald Loe of Roosevelt, L.I., New York, who helped organize churches in various parts of the country and served important Association churches; and the Rev. Irving Halleen, formerly of Boone, Iowa, now of Wheaton, Illinois, who was twice moderator of the Evangelical Free Church of America and an active leader in the Ministerial Association and other phases of the Free Church. (At the time of this writing Mr. Halleen, at 91 years of age, is still living, and until four years ago was teaching an older people's Bible class in the Evangelical Free Church of Wheaton.)

The special issue included an article by former editor Roy Thompson on "Ten Major Events in Free Church History," a story about Mr. C. A. Johnson of Boone, Iowa, who, at 93, was believed to be the only living person who attended the Evangelical

Free Church conference in Boone in 1884. (He was an honorary delegate at the Jubilee conference in Denver.) An article on the beginnings of the work of the Evangelical Free Church Association in Boston, another on the church at Boone, Iowa, and testimonies by former Free Church men now serving in other areas (Dr. Raymond I. Lindquist, Dr. Torrey M. Johnson, Rev. Bernt C. Opsal and Evangelist Mervin Rosell) were of special interest. Ken Anderson's article, "Grandmother Taught Me Much" paid tribute to a godly Free Church home. Billy Graham sent a greeting through the *Beacon* and mentioned that some of his closest friends and some of God's greatest Christians were reared in Evangelical Free Church homes. The daughter of Free Church president Arnold Olson (now a medical doctor) and a grandson of Dr. E. A. Halleen (now a Presbyterian minister) wrote inspiring articles on "The Free Church of Tomorrow." The back page of this 32-page issue carried the Free Church doctrinal statement, "What the Evangelical Free Church Believes," a document that has been felt to explain one reason for the effectiveness of the EFCA impact.

As the Diamond Jubilee year came to an end, there was the announcement in the December 29 issue of the *Beacon* by Dr. Olson of the conference theme for 1960—DEEPER YET. He reminded his readers that there was still "much land yet to be possessed," and that "before we move on, it would be well to stop and consolidate our gains, check up on our lines of communication, and remind one another of the oft-repeated but easily forgotten truth that *we cannot go farther until we have first gone deeper!*"

THREE

OVERSEAS MISSIONS

A DECADE OF ADVANCE ON OUR OVERSEAS MISSION FIELDS

The theme of our Diamond Jubilee conference—"Forward in the Faith of Our Fathers"—may well sum up and characterize the Overseas Missions outreach of the Evangelical Free Church of America during the past ten years. Facing the unfinished task of carrying out the Great Commission, our leaders have literally re-doubled their efforts and program in taking the message of the Gospel to the seven overseas mission fields for which our denomination is responsible.

It is exactly ten years ago that the director of our overseas mission, Dr. Lester Westlund, presented his first annual report. Succeeding the Rev. H. G. Rodine, who held this post for twelve years, Dr. Westlund has directed the work during the past decade in the zeal and in the faith of those pioneer leaders of our work who have always given top priority to the cause of foreign missions.

One way to measure the growth of the missionary enterprise over a given period is to look at the financial reports. The income for foreign missions reported at our Diamond Jubilee conference, ten years ago, was $402,000. Nine years later this figure had almost exactly doubled, to $806,000. Budgeted for the 1968-69 fiscal year was the sum of $825,000.

While this higher figure reflects the higher *cost* of maintaining and promoting the missionary enterprise on the seven mission fields, it also indicates a broadening and intensifying of the missionary program around the world—the new thrusts in training the converts for Gospel work, the new emphasis in medical missions, the more vigorous program of planting new churches on the various fields, and the building of suitable chapels and churches and Gospel centers.

Ten years ago our Evangelical Free churches were supporting 149 missionaries working under our Overseas Mission board. There were 69 in the Congo, 4 in Venezuela, 14 in Japan, 12 in Hong Kong, eight in the Philippines, four in Malaysia, and two in Germany.

Nine years later, in 1968, the total number of missionaries under the EFCA board was 162, with 49 assigned to Congo, 50 to Venezuela, 19 to Hong Kong, 20 to Japan, 15 to the Philippines, six to Malaysia, and three to Germany.

This is by no means the sum total of foreign missionary work carried on by our Evangelical Free churches. A survey made by Dr. Westlund two years ago came up with the astounding report that more than 500 men and women brought up in our Evangelical Free churches were serving as missionaries under various organizations other than the Evangelical Free Church. For the past several years the number of Free Church missionaries serving under the Evangelical Alliance Mission (TEAM) has been almost a hundred. These are receiving the greater portion of their support from our Evangelical Free churches.

A brief survey of what has been taking place during the past ten years on our seven fields will illustrate the forward movement that has been experienced.

THE REPUBLIC OF CONGO

A crisis was pending on our Congo field at conference time in 1960. What had been the Belgian Congo for 52 years was to become the Republic of Congo on July 1, an independent and sovereign nation. The future of our work there was unpredictable, according to Dr. Westlund, who urged our people to pray definitely for the 63 missionaries and 55 missionary children on the Congo staff. The July 26 issue of the *Beacon* announced in big, black capital letters on the cover page:

MISSIONARIES LEAVE CONGO

39 MISSIONARIES, 36 CHILDREN ALL SAFE IN MAJOR EVACUATION. THREE MEN REMAIN ON FIELD, OTHER MEN RETURN AFTER WOMEN HEAD HOME. FIRST ARRIVALS REACH AMERICA ON TUESDAY, JULY 19. AIR FORCE GLOBEMASTER USED TO FLY WOMEN, CHILDREN TO FRANKFURT.

Eleven men returned to the field after the first evacuation and reported that conditions were quiet and that there was a minimum of anti-white feeling at the time. None of the mission property had been damaged. A cable urged that more of the missionaries return to the field. The schools were to open on schedule and the native leaders were asking for help to continue the work.

The crisis in Congo resulted in the turning over of the mission work to the Evangelical Church of the Ubangi, with most of the leadership and responsibility placed in the hands of the native leaders, such as already had been done in our Venezuela and Hong Kong fields.

Though conditions were quite unstable during the first years of Congo's independence, the work continued and more and more of our missionaries were able to return to the field.

Dr. Titus Johnson, founder of our Congo mission, was in Congo at the time of the revolution. He had some hair-raising experiences, described in his book, *When Congo Burst Its Seams*, edited by Mel Larson and published by Free Church Publications, but escaped those who sought to kill him and remained a year after "independence" working under the United Nations and serving in half a dozen hospitals where doctors were scarce and needs were most urgent.

Late in 1962, Dr. Westlund reported, after a visit to the field, that the national church was "maturing" and carrying on in a commendable manner and that the national leaders were most appreciative of the assistance rendered by our missionaries.

There were disturbances in Congo again in 1964 which necessitated the temporary evacuation of our missionaries to nearby Bangui, in the Central African Republic. Rebel forces were advancing closer to the area where our work is located and it was considered advisable for them to leave. This is the year that Dr. Paul Carlson, Covenant missionary doctor, was killed.

The hospital at Tandala was re-opened in 1965-66 and the secondary schools were "in full swing." More than 3,000 had professed Christ as Savior during the year, bringing the total membership of the churches in Congo to 22,000.

The big news on the field in 1966 was the arrival of a Cessna 185 plane to facilitate travel on the part of the missionaries and workers. It is flown by an M.A.F. pilot.

Conditions were quite stable by 1967 and the native church had been growing. It was estimated that some 32,000 people were attending church regularly at the various stations. More than 600 had professed Christ in the hospital and dispensaries. More than 36,000 people had been treated in the clinics.

A full-scale theological seminary was in the planning stage, according to a report to our 1968 conference. At the end of the year there was rejoicing on the part of our Overseas Missions staff that prayer had been answered in filling a desperate need for a doctor for our hospital at Tandala. Dr. Van Ness, the only doctor there at the beginning of 1969, wrote that our hospital was the only facility for providing medical care for 200,000 to 300,000 people.

Three leaders from the national church in Congo have visited our churches and conferences in the homeland during the past five years and have brought much blessing and inspiration. They are the Rev. Isaac Pelendo, veteran saint and preacher, who spent the summer of 1964 in our country visiting our churches and taking part in the 80th annual conference of the EFCA at Ocean Grove, New Jersey; the Rev. Zacharie Alenge, president of the Evangelical Church of the Ubangi, in 1965, who likewise endeared himself to our people as he visited our churches and conferences; and the Rev. Luke Saba, pastor and youth leader, whose presence and participation in our 1968 conference at Trinity thrilled our people.

HONG KONG

Miracles have taken place in our Hong Kong field during the past decade, foremost of which were the erection and dedication of a modern hospital and a beautiful new building for the Evangel Children's Home.

Referring to the hospital project, Rev. Robert Dillon, associate director of our Overseas Missions department, commented in *The Evangelical Beacon*, "We have seen more miracles in connection with this project than in any other we have known about."

There was the miracle of the grant of land for this purpose by the Hong Kong government—a half-acre plot in an ideal location worth at least $300,000. Another answer to prayer was a grant of $85,000 from the Far East Refugee Program of the United States Department of State.

It seems that the entire project evolved in a manner that was "exceeding abundantly above all one could ask or think." Dr. Robert Chapman and Dr. Gordon Addington had gone to Hong Kong to set up a modest clinic, but hadn't been there very long until they recognized the need for a real hospital facility. In consultation with Evangelical Free Church leaders, they dared to plan for a 45-bed modern hospital and to pray for the money with which to build and equip it.

The editorial announcement in the Beacon on March 2, 1965, that the hospital had been dedicated on February 28 and that the $558,000 structure had been completed and was *debt-free,* seemed almost too good to be true. There was recognition of the fact that "This is the Lord's doing; it is marvellous in our eyes."

During the first year of operation, the hospital admitted 647 patients and also treated more than 15,000 in the clinic.

The second "miracle" in our Hong Kong field was the dedication of a new Children's Home in 1963. For years our workers had done their best to care for as many homeless children as possible with the limited and inadequate facilities they had, but had prayed that God would provide something bigger and better to meet this need. Now the prayer was finally answered through the generosity of the Rev. and Mrs. Wilbur E. Nelson of the Morning Chapel Hour, who had for some years been supporting the Home and who now had taken as a special project the raising of money for the erection of a new Evangel Children's Home.

Erected at a cost of some $80,000, the beautiful and spacious new Evangel Children's Home was presented to our Mission by the Morning Chapel Hour in 1963. Helping to dedicate the Home were the Rev. and Mrs. Wilbur E. Nelson whose presence and participation in the festivities made the occasion a highlight for our entire missionary staff, as well as for the workers in the Home.

A third special event or development in our Hong Kong field during the past few years has been the "evolution" of our Bible Institute into the Evangel Theological College, which graduated its first class of 16 in 1967. The Canton Bible Institute, organized more than thirty years ago by the late Rev. Arthur G. Lindquist, had served well in training hundreds of young people for Christian service, but there was definite need of upgrading the school to approach the level of a theological seminary, and this has now been accomplished.

The work of our Evangel Press and Evangel Book Store continues to grow as they produce, publish and sell large quantities of Christian literature.

There are six organized churches in Hong Kong where 19 missionaries were at work in 1967. Six national pastors serve these churches, which have a membership of nearly 1,400. The Chinese church totally supports its own program and also supports a missionary, Rev. James Wong, who has been serving with our mission in Malaysia. The Grace Church, which operates its own clinic, is also supporting its first foreign missionary, Miss Olivia Haw, who has gone to Thailand to work with the Wycliffe Translators.

VENEZUELA

This is now our largest field so far as personnel is concerned, where we have 52 missionaries on the staff. There are 23 organized and five unorganized churches with a total membership of 850. All of the churches except three are served by national pastors. Our missionaries have turned over the responsibility to the nationals and helped them to establish a strong national church that is self-supporting. The churches are now supporting their first missionaries, the Raga family, who have gone to minister to the Indians on the Brazilian border.

Our Bible Institute at El Limon has trained a considerable number of natives for the pastorate and developed a splendid campus in this suburb of the large city of Maracay. The campus is now being made ready for the launching of a full-scale theological seminary, to be operated in cooperation with the Evangelical Alliance Mission (TEAM).

In cooperation with TEAM, a printing establishment and publishing house has been established at Maracaibo, turning out millions of copies of Gospel tracts and other Christian literature. A quarterly magazine, *Orientacion,* geared to professional people, is being published and is finding an excellent response from many to whom the magazine is sent.

A missionary children's dormitory has been built, near El Limon. A national school for children, fully accredited, has been in operation at Maracay for the past seven years. A more recent project is the establishment of an orphanage, also at Maracay.

Unable to build the radio station which the Women's Missionary Society had raised money for, the missionaries are using various secular stations for broadcasting the Gospel. During one recent year they reported having used 422 hours of radio time in sending forth the message of the Gospel.

Our missionaries are at present deeply involved in a "Caracas for Christ" program. With financial help from the Women's Missionary Society, our workers are aiming to establish at least five new churches in this great metropolis of 2,000,000 people during the next five years. The Evangelism in Depth program, in which our workers participated, reached thousands of people who had not previously been reached, and our missionaries are bending every effort to carry on in the spirit of consecration that characterized that united effort on the part of all evangelical groups in the country.

The visit of national leaders from the field always stimulates new interest and prayer for the work. During the past decade two such leaders have visited the United States and spent the better part of a year studying at Trinity Evangelical Divinity School and visiting our churches and conferences. The Rev. José Liscano came in 1959 and endeared himself to our people as he visited in the churches and took part in the Diamond Jubilee conference at Denver. More recently one of the younger pastors from the field, Rev. Manuel Suarez, and his family spent the entire school year of 1967-68 at Trinity, also singing and preaching in many of our churches.

JAPAN

The radio ministry of our missionaries here has been paying off during the past few years. Begun by Dr. Calvin Hanson, who pioneered our work in Japan, this work has continued through the years. No less than 1,460 people responded to 13 hours of Gospel broadcasting in a recent count, many of whom have been led to the Lord.

There are nine organized churches and seven other preaching points where at least 500 people are in attendance on any Lord's

Day. Actual membership was close to 350 in 1967. Attendance at Bible camp last summer exceeded 300 boys and girls.

An indication that the nationals are realizing their own responsibility for carrying on missionary work is that our churches in Japan have sent out and are supporting their own first foreign missionary. Miss Sumi Yokouchi has served as a missionary on our Malaysia field and was home on her first furlough last year.

The newly established Gospel centers, made possible by the Women's Missionary Society project in 1964, have been an effective means of winning the lost. Mrs. Reuben Strombeck, president of the Women's Missionary Society, visited the Japan field last fall and saw the church at Kawaguche, erected with funds from the project. She was entertained in the missionary residence in Kyoto, provided by W.M.S. funds. She was impressed by the strategy used by our missionaries in inviting the Japanese to their homes for classes in English (which the Japanese are so eager to learn). As some of these become converts they form the nuclei in the formation of new churches.

One of the national leaders of our work in Japan is the Rev. Andrew Furuyama, remembered by our people in the homeland, who learned to know and love him in 1962 when he spent a year studying at Trinity and taking part in our churches and conferences with much blessing.

THE PHILIPPINES

The work in the Philippine Islands was just getting started ten years ago. Located on the island of Cebu, our 16 missionaries are laboring in Cebu City and in the southern part of the island.

By 1962, two chapels had been built by the national church. A good camping program was in progress by 1963 and arrangements were made the following year to purchase a suitable site for the camping program.

Our missionaries are cooperating with the Far Eastern Gospel Crusade in establishing and maintaining the Central Bible Training Institute in Cebu City, where several of our workers are teaching and assisting in other ways. They are also cooperating with the newly organized Philippines Sunday School Publications and have assigned one missionary to work full-time on this project.

As of 1967 there were three organized churches and another four unorganized churches and four other preaching points. There are about 100 members and about 200 in the Sunday schools. Tent campaigns are conducted which attract large crowds. Thirty-six hours of radio broadcasting in one year brought a fairly good response. A youth center is being used to reach university students, and an English-speaking church is developing in Cebu City that should, in the future, be the center of our Cebu work.

Dr. Westlund reported at our 1968 conference that a National Evangelical Free Church had now been organized. This has been the goal on all our foreign mission fields, which goal has now been reached with the organization of the work on this basis in the Philippines.

MALAYSIA

Ten years ago the work in Singapore and Malaysia, our sixth field, was just getting started. The Eric McMurrays arrived, via a cargo vessel from Canada, during the summer of 1958 to take over a work that had its small beginning through the efforts of the Rev. and Mrs. Arthur G. Lindquist, from our Hong Kong field, the previous year. The Lindquists stayed on long enough to assist in the establishment of the work in Singapore.

By 1959 five stations had been opened in the city and a chapel-residence rented and furnished which provided a headquarters for the Malaya work.

A second couple, the Ben Sawatskys, had joined the staff by the summer of 1961, when it was possible to report that there was already an organized church with about 100 in attendance and eight Sunday schools with a total attendance of about 275.

The chapel-residence that had been rented in 1959 was purchased in 1962 and another church started in a different area.

A youth conference and a literature conference had been held and the *Malayan Beacon* launched to keep our constituency fully informed with respect to the progress of the work.

Another couple, the James Phalens, was added to the staff in 1964 and a goal of "a new church in each of the 14 states comprising Malaysia in the next five years" was set by the young missionaries and the national churches of Singapore.

.A correspondence school was commenced which has met with an amazing response. One advertisement in a leading newspaper brought in more than 600 applications. More than 2,000 have enrolled in courses being offered by the mission.

As of conference time in 1968 we had only three missionary couples in our Malaysia field, namely, the Ben Sawatskys, the Richard Carlsons, and the Allen Tunbergs. It had been necessary for the McMurrays and the Phalens to return to the homeland for various reasons.

Our missionaries took an active part in the recent Asian Congress on Evangelism at Singapore, where twelve official delegates from three Evangelical Free Church fields in the Far East were present—four each from Japan, Hong Hong, and Malaysia and Singapore. The Congress afforded "an unprecedented opportunity for EFC leaders in Asia, both national and missionary, to meet together," writes Ben Sawatsky in the January 28, 1969 issue of the *Beacon.* As of now we have three organized churches and one unorganized church in the field. Six young people are in Bible school or seminary. The church membership is about 125, with nearly 600 attending on Sundays. Sunday school enrollment is about 330.

GERMANY

The work in Germany has not progressed as was expected when it was started 11 years ago. It started with a great deal of enthusiasm, and the report presented to our conference in 1959 was most encouraging, though we had only two workers there at the time.

Another couple joined the staff in 1960, one couple working in Gandersheim, in the northeast corner of West Germany.

The 1961 report indicated that the work was progressing, with regular services being held in six different towns and occasional meetings in several others.

A Bible Institute and Camp building was purchased in 1962, dedicated in August, with plans for establishing a Bible Institute. The Bible Institute opened in the fall of 1963 with the Rev. Henry G. Rempel, formerly of Steinbach, Manitoba, as the director.

The work in Germany has been reorganized since 1965. It was found expedient to work in closer cooperation with the German Free Evangelical Church, which was desiring to establish a Bible Institute program. Three of our workers on the field were assigned to assist the German church in the Bible Institute. In addition, a thriving church has been started in Osterode. The first class was graduated from the Bible Institute in 1968.

Visiting our 1968 conference at Trinity last summer were two leaders of the German Free Evangelical Church, one of whom, Rev. Wilhelm Gilbert, president of the denomination, was honored by Trinity with a Doctor of Divinity degree. The other visitor was the Rev. Carl Heinz Knoppel.

As of conference time a year ago only three missionaries were working in Germany under the Evangelical Free Church Overseas Mission Board, namely, Rev. and Mrs. David Henrichs and Miss Martha Goertzen.

FOUR

HOME MISSIONS

EXPANSION ON THE HOME FIELD

The only basic difference between home missions and foreign missions is that one is occupied with evangelizing in the home country and the other with what has been considered "foreign" countries. Witnessing "in Jerusalem, and in Judea, and in Samaria" has been considered "home missions," while witnessing "to the uttermost part of the earth" has been called "foreign" or "overseas" missions. Otherwise the objectives are the same; namely, to "make disciples of all nations . . . teaching them to observe all things" which the Lord of the Harvest has commanded.

Ten years ago, at our Diamond Jubilee conference, the Rev. Olai Urang, who had served as home mission secretary for ten years, presented his last report to the conference, inasmuch as he was to leave in the fall to become superintendent of the Eastern District Association. The year had been one of the best in the history of the Evangelical Free Church from the standpoint of growth, 34 churches having been added to our fellowship during the year.

Succeeding Mr. Urang was the Rev. Herbert E. Kyrk, who had had both good training and good experience for the kind of work to which he had been called. In close cooperation with the superintendents of the various District conferences, he continued to promote an aggressive program of expansion of our Evangelical Free Church work in the United States and Canada. His report to our 1960 conference included some new features, such as the home missions institute conducted at Trinity College and Trinity Evangelical Divinity School, "to present the problems, challenges and victories of home missions and to maintain a close rapport between the schools and the districts." These institutes, attended by District superintendents as well as the home mission secretary, have been conducted year after year during the past decade with much blessing and visible fruit. In his report to our 1968 conference Mr. Kyrk said that between 35 and 40 members of the graduating class in our divinity school had expressed an interest in serving the Lord in our Evangelical Free Church field.

The Home Mission department has taken the initiative in establishing churches outside the territory of any of our District associations, such as the church in the Washington, D. C. area, at Arlington, Va., authorized by the Evangelical Free Church conference in 1960. This church, started by the Rev. Olai Urang, who had moved to the East Coast, became self-supporting two years after its organization.

Three other churches were sponsored by the Home Mission department in 1961 and 1962 which were outside the jurisdiction of any District society—at Hurricane, West Virginia; another in Magog, Quebec, and still another in Phoenix, Arizona. These churches have prospered. The church at Phoenix, like the one at Arlington, Va., became self-supporting in two years.

As the church in Phoenix grew, its horizons were widened and it helped to establish two other churches in the state, one at Tucson and one at Tempe, where the University of Arizona is located.

In 1963 our Home Mission department launched what it called "Operation-Cooperation Evangelism" (O.C.E.), which employed teams of students from our colleges and Divinity school for service to our churches and Districts in Bible camp work, Vacation Bible schools, Sunday schools, and youth work. Several teams were sent out during each of five summers. Expenses were underwritten by the Home Mission department. The program was well received by the churches, but after five years the Home Mission department felt it could no longer bear the expense of the program, which had resulted in a deficit of more than $26,000. The program is now directed by our schools.

Sensing a need of greater evangelistic endeavors, the Home Mission department, in 1964, engaged one of our successful pastors, the Rev. Joy C. Cummings, as a full-time evangelist, to work under the sponsorship of the department. His "family-type crusades," with a strong appeal to children and young people, have been used of the Lord in reaching and winning hundreds of children and young people to the Lord. His crusades are so popular that as of last fall he was already booked for crusades through May of 1969.

Still another evangelist was engaged by the Home Mission department in 1966 when the Rev. Jake Reinhardt, formerly one of our Free Church missionaries to Germany, began an evangelistic ministry among our churches in the United States and Canada. Last summer he launched what was called "A New Thrust in Visitation Evangelism." A feature article in the September 24, 1968 issue of *The Evangelical Beacon* described the program he directed at the Salem Free Church of Minneapolis over a period of several months. Carefully and prayerfully planned, the systematic visitation of homes in the community resulted in a number of definite conversions among people who never would have attended an evangelistic service in a church.

The Shareholders program, by means of which new churches are helped by substantial grants for their building programs, was inaugurated in 1952. This program has been stepped up during the past decade, with more persons participating (a 1,400 increase in 1962), resulting in a larger grant to the churches. There have been four such projects during each of the past seven years, the grants to each church varying between $6,000 and $8,000. The 50th church to be helped in this way was the new congregation at Wikiup, Calif. (about an hour's drive north of San Francisco), where seven acres of land have been purchased for the establishment of an Evangelical Free church in an area where no church of any denomination is now working. An architect's sketch of the proposed edifice appeared in the *Beacon* of November 5, 1968.

Income to the Home Mission department was less than $50,000 for the fiscal year ended April 30, 1959. Nine years later, on April 30, 1968, it was possible to report an income for the year of more than $137,000—an indication of the expansion of the services rendered by the Home Mission department during the past decade.

The newest ventures sponsored by the Home Mission department are the new churches established in Alaska and Hawaii, the last two states to become a part of the United States of America.

Rev. and Mrs. Robert Hoobyar, with a burden for souls in Alaska, after visiting the field, and after visiting at least a hundred churches, sharing their burden with them, went to the field in the fall of 1966 and established a work at Fairbanks. The following summer they were able to report that a church had been organized with 14 charter members, with an attendance of 39 in the morning services and 44 in the Sunday school. A devastating flood in the summer of 1967 caused considerable damage to the property, much of which was replaced with help from an emergency flood fund. Growth of the work has continued in spite of the setback, so that at our conference last year it could be reported that the average attendance was 55, with 63 in the Sunday school and 44 at evening services, and 21 at prayer meeting.

The work in Hawaii is in its infancy, but the prospects for a strong church there are exceedingly favorable. The Rev. Ben C. Erickson, pastor for twelve years of the First Evangelical Free Church of St. Paul, an Air Force Reserve chaplain, went to the field last summer and has established a work in Honolulu. First services were held in the early fall with more than forty people in attendance, including Chaplain (Col.) Mervin Johnson, Evangelical Free Church chaplain in Hawaii; a medical doctor and his family from the Summerdale church in Chicago, Dr. Warren Anderson, who is assigned to Tripler Army Hospital in Honolulu, and many others who have been active in Evangelical Free churches in the States. As a reserve chaplain, Pastor Erickson also has opportunity to minister to Air Force personnel and their dependents at the Tripler Hospital.

The year 1967, when the Dominion of Canada was celebrating its centennial, the Evangelical Free churches of British Columbia, Alberta, Saskatchewan and Manitoba observed their Golden Jubilee, commemorating the beginning of the work at Enchant, Alberta, in June of 1917.

The Golden Jubilee Conference, held at Calgary March 28-31, brought 150 pastors and delegates from the seventy cooperating churches together for the occasion, along with President Arnold Olson, Home Mission Secretary Herbert Kyrk, the Rev. Olai Urang (one of the pioneers in the Canadian field) and others from the States.

In preparation for the event, Mrs. Calvin Hanson wrote a fascinating story of the Canadian work, *Fifty Years and Seventy Places*. An inspiring program had been prepared for the conference.

A business session brought about the reorganization of the Canadian work as *The Evangelical Free Church of Canada,* with a set of officers and a Board of Directors for the newly formed corporation.

Climax of the conference was reached during a banquet attended by 547 people when Dr. Robert N. Thompson, member of Parliament from Ottawa, presented a Dominion Charter to Dr. Olson, who in turn presented it to the Rev. Carl Fosmark, who had been elected chairman of the new organization.

Secretary of Home Missions Herbert Kyrk explained that the formation of the Evangelical Free Church of Canada "will greatly facilitate the easy movement of our organization from province to province in Canada, which will now be able to extend itself into all of the Dominion with the Gospel of Christ without any legal restrictions." He also makes it clear that "the new organization is still just as much a part of the Evangelical Free Church of America as it ever has been."

Home Mission Secretary Herbert Kyrk reported at our 1967 conference that "a dramatic step of faith" had been taken by the Western District, which had become so large that it seemed expedient to divide it. The Southwest District was formed to include the greater Los Angeles area and all of southern California and Arizona. Dr. Herbert Peterson, who has been superintendent of the Western District for many years, serves the northern California churches and the churches of Nevada. Mr. Kyrk is hopeful that other large districts will take this as an "example for doing the work of the Lord more efficiently." He is also burdened to see Evangelical Free churches started in parts of the country where no such testimony now exists.

Motivated by the desire to extend the influence of the Evangelical Free Church in areas where our denomination is not known, Mr. Kyrk has prepared an attractive brochure entitled "What Others Say About Us," in which there are quotes from former Premier Ernest C. Manning of Alberta, Canada; Rev. Leighton Ford, associate evangelist of the Billy Graham Association; Dr. Harold J. Ockenga, pastor of the famous Park Street Church of Boston, Mass.; Dr. William Culbertson, president of Moody Bible Institute; Dr. Jack Wyrtzen, director of Word of Life Fellowship; Dr. Clyde Taylor, executive secretary of the National Association of Evangelicals; Dr. Theodore H. Epp, director of Back to the Bible Broadcast; Dick Hillis, general director of Overseas Crusades; Al Worthington, pitcher for the Minnesota Twins baseball club; Sam Wolgemuth, president, Youth for Christ, International; Dr. Clyde Narramore, director, Narramore Christian Foundation, and Dr. J. Vernon McGee, pastor of the Church of the Open Door of Los Angeles. All of these indicate their wholehearted appreciation of the ministry of the Evangelical Free Church of America and its role in promoting "the faith once for all delivered unto the saints."

FIVE

PUBLICATIONS

PAVING THE WAY FOR ADVANCEMENT

Secretary of Publications John Walkup, reporting to the 1968 conference, quoted Dr. E. A. Halleen, former president of the EFCA, in reminding our constituency that "the publications pave the way for advancement." Throughout the entire 85-year history of our denomination, this has been true, and not least during the past decade of almost unparalleled advancement. The importance of the Publication department was confirmed by a court decision in 1963, at which time we were seeking a continuation of the tax-exempt status of our printing concern and book store. The court ruled that our denomination was dependent on its publication department in carrying out the purposes for which the denomination exists.

Changes have been made in the Publication department during the past decade. The need for larger and more adequate space was obvious when the report of the Publication department was presented to the Diamond Jubilee conference ten years ago. The conference was reminded that the "Blueprint for Progress" that had been prepared in connection with the Diamond Jubilee observance had included as one of its goals "the development and extension of all the tangible facilities which increase our effectiveness in spreading the Gospel."

When the mortgage on the property at 2950 Nicollet Ave. (which had served as headquarters for both the administrative offices and the publication department since the merger of 1950) was paid off, through Jubilee Funds in April of 1960, a committee appointed by the Executive Committee of the EFCA had already been looking for a suitable site for the erection of a new headquarters and publication building. A resolution presented by the Board of Publications at our 1960 conference recommended that "action be taken as soon as possible" to provide adequate housing for the headquarters and publication department.

The following summer authorization was given by the conference to proceed with the construction of the new building on the site already acquired, plans for which had been prepared.

The dedication of the building, of brick and Kasota stone in contemporary architecture, at 1515 E. 66th Street in Richfield (a few blocks south of the Minneapolis city limits), on October 6, 1962, was called by Editor Mel Larson "a historic milestone in the many-pronged outreach of our Evangelical Free Church."

Since approximately 75 per cent of the finished space in the new building is occupied by the Publication department (book store, press, publications, editorial offices and office of the Secretary of Publications), the department has been paying its proportionate share of the monthly mortgage payments and cost of maintaining and operating the building. Meeting this obligation has posed no great problem since both the book store and press have operated at a modest profit during almost all of the years since the building was completed.

There have been changes in the personnel of the department during the past decade. After 38 years of service to the Evangelical Free Church in a publications ministry, Roy A. Thompson was retired as Secretary of Publications on July 1, 1964. After turning over the editorship of *The Evangelical Beacon* (of which he had been editor for 27 years) to Mel Larson, he served as Secretary of Publications from 1958 until his retirement in 1964.

Mel Larson assumed the responsibilities as Acting Secretary of Publicaitons from July 1, 1964 until June 1, 1966, when Mr. Chester Gunderson, member of the Board of Publications, took over until September, when the Rev. John W. Walkup assumed the office on an interim appointment by the Executive Board pending his nomination for a three-year term at the 1967 conference.

Happily there has been no need for any change of personnel so far as *The Evangelical Beacon* is concerned, nor in the management of the Beacon Book Store.

There has been steady growth and progress and improvement in *The Evangelical Beacon* since Mr. Mel Larson became editor in 1958. That year the *Beacon* was being sent to almost 13,000 homes each week. By November 19, 1968—just a decade later—the circulation had almost doubled, having climbed to 25,000! We question if any other denomination of comparable size has a circulation of its official magazine as large as this. One reason for the large circulation is the success of the circulation campaigns in getting nearly 400 of our churches to subscribe for their member families and constituency on the so-called "budget plan."

Another reason, of course, is the excellence of the editorial job being done by our editor and his assistant, Mrs. Edwin Groenhoff. Awards have been made to the *Beacon* by the Evangelical Press Association on several occasions for outstanding features that have enhanced the effectiveness of the magazine. During the past ten years there have been changes in the design and format of the paper on several occasions. More and more color is being used in improving the attractiveness of the paper. Again and again there have been unsolicited comments by other-than-Free Church people that we have one of the finest denominational magazines in the country.

The biggest change during the past decade was the change from 16 pages every week to 32 pages every other week. A survey in the fall of 1963 showed that a great majority of the subscribers favored such a change. The change made possible a still greater improvement in the contents and effectiveness of the journal, with more and more color being used and more pictures.

The Beacon Book Store has also been under the same management during the past decade, and the excellent management provided by Mr. Donald C. Brower has given our Evangelical Free Church of America one of the best and one of the most successful Christian book stores in the Upper Midwest. Sales increased from $162,000 in the 1958-59 fiscal year to $272,000 during the fiscal year ended last April, 1968. Without exception there have been substantial net profits, which have made possible tens of thousands of dollars in contributions to other Free Church enterprises, such as *The Evangelical Beacon,* the Sunday School or Christian Education department, the Overseas Mission department, Free Church Publications, etc.

Free Church Press has had its ups and downs during the past ten years. The report of the manager to our conference in 1959 appeared to be one of the most encouraging we had ever seen up to that time. The following year, however, showed the biggest deficit ever reported. We were happy for the coming of the Rev. Darrell (Bud) Pearson to manage the shop in the fall of 1960 and felt he was the answer to some of the problems in the shop. He served as manager almost six years until May 1, 1966, when he left to serve fulltime as pastor of the Evangelical Free Church of Edina, Minn., which he had helped to establish and which he had served' on a part-time basis for some time previously. His last year as manager was one of the best, with a volume of sales amounting to $230,000, and a modest net profit. There was constant improvement in the quality of work done and in the facilities of the shop. The Every Sunday Bulletin service provided for our Evangelical Free churches reached a new high in both quantity and quality.

The present manager is Mr. Glen Johnson, who took over the management when Mr. Pearson left, and who came back again as manager, after two years with another concern, after Mr. David Simning's two-year term as manager. The two years of Mr. Simning's management were especially good from the standpoint of total sales, shop morale, and net operating profits.

Next to the ministry of *The Evangelical Beacon,* perhaps the greatest service rendered to the Evangelical Free Church constituency and the evangelical cause in general during the past ten years has been in the publication and sale of about 25 books and tens of thousands of Gospel tracts.

The publication of the *Diamond Jubilee Story* ten years ago was the most ambitious project undertaken up to that time. The 335-page history, of which 4,400 copies were printed and sold, made its important contribution to the work. Now out of print, it has just appeared in a paperback edition for the benefit of newer people in the Evangelical Free Church who desire to know the history of their denomination from the beginning. The volume in your hands now is a supplement to the *Diamond Jubilee Story,* published as a separate book in view of the exciting progress made during this past decade of advancement along all lines.

The publication of President Arnold Olson's large volume, *This We Believe,* was the most important publishing project of 1961 and has met a very urgent need in explaining what the Evangelical Free Church believes and why. A second printing of the book, in 1965, added features that improved the usefulness of the book. A condensed edition of the book, in 12 lessons, has been used in Bible classes and Bible instruction courses.

Published in 1964, Dr. Olson's 367-page volume, *Believers Only,* is an outline of the history and principles of the Free Evangelical denominations in Europe and North America affiliated with the International Federation of Free Evangelical Churches.

Throughout almost the entire past decade a large number of our pastors have used in their Bible instruction classes an 80-page catechism prepared by Roy A. Thompson in 1960 entitled *Essen-*

tials of the Christian Faith. This project was initiated by the Ministerial Association which elected a committee of mature pastors with whom Mr. Thompson conferred in the writing of the book. It has been necessary to print several editions of the book to meet the demand until such time as a more ambitious series of handbooks can be made available to our pastors.

You and Your Church has served our churches as a kind of membership manual since the first edition appeared ten years ago. Nearly 20,000 copies of the book have been printed including the sixth edition, revised, which has recently appeared.

A Minister's Service Manual, in loose-leaf form, has provided our pastors with the kind of handbook they need for weddings, funerals, dedications, etc.

When Congo Burst Its Seams, by Dr. Titus Johnson (as told to Mel Larson) and *Pelendo, God's Prophet in the Congo,* by Mrs. Richard B. Anderson, have had a wide circulation, not only among Free Church people but in many other groups as well.

Marjorie Soderholm's little booklet, *Explaining Salvation to Children,* has been reprinted again and again to meet the demand. Now in its seventh edition, the total number of copies sold is approaching 30,000. The sequel on the followup of the child convert, *Salvation, Then What?,* published in the fall of 1968, is gaining recognition as a unique and important book on this neglected theme.

Prof. John E. Dahlin's *Prophetic Truth for Today* has also had to be reprinted several times in order to meet the need of clear and sane and sound teaching on the subject of Biblical prophecy.

Our Publication department printed 20,000 copies of Dr. Wilbur M. Smith's 64-page volume on *The Incomparable Book* to encourage people to "Read It Through in '62."

Mel Larson's *114 Ways to the Mission Field,* a sequel to his *117 Ways to the Mission Field,* has met with an excellent response, as have his books for teen-agers, *Everybody's Not Doing It,* and *Yardstick For Youth.*

Dr. Edwin Groenhoff's *Psalms for Cloudy Days,* beautifully il-lustrated, in its three editions, has been a source of great encour-agement and comfort to thousands of people. His smaller book, *So You're Going to College,* has been a challenge to hundreds of young people.

Other books and booklets published during the past decade are *Forward in the Faith of Our Fathers; This is Your Life,* by Dr. T. B. Madsen; *From a Shepherd's Heart,* by Rev. Gustaf F. John-son; *Honey and Salt* and *Fifty Years and Seventy Places* (history of our Canadian churches), by Muriel Hanson; *Long Shadow,* a biography of Carl Gundersen by his wife; *The Revelation of Jesus Christ,* by Rev. Leonard E. Hagstrom; *Neither Right Nor Left,* by Dr. Arnold Olson, and *Why Join a Church?,* also by Dr. Olson, and a reprint of Dr. C. T. Dyrness's *Bible Truths.*

A quarterly newsletter, *Freelines,* prepared by Secretary of Publications John Walkup, sent to bookstores to promote the sale of Free Church publications, also keeps the pastors and leaders of our Evangelical Free Church informed as to what is happening in the far-reaching ministry of the printed page by means of the Beacon Book Store, Free Church Press, Free Church Publications, and the denominational magazine, *The Evangelical Beacon.*

The Publications department continues to make a real effort to fulfill its role to *pave the way* for further advancement. A revolv-ing fund to facilitate the financing of new books and tracts was started in 1965 with a deposit of $3,000.00 and reached $10,-001.01 early in 1969. As the fiscal year drew to a close a new larger press costing $31,000.00 was installed. Earlier in the year another investment was made in equipment costing $14,553.20. The last volume to be printed on the old press was Elmer Towns' optimistic title, *The Bright Future of Sunday School.* Appro-priately, the first book to be printed on the new press is the one you are reading, *Toward New Horizons.* The doubled *Evangelical Beacon* circulation, nearing the 26,000 mark, was being produced on the new equipment at twice the former speed.

SIX

CHRISTIAN EDUCATION

AN EXPANDED CHRISTIAN EDUCATION PROGRAM

The principal development in the area of Christian Education during the past decade has been the transformation of the Sunday School department into a full-scale Christian Education department, not limited to the program of the Sunday school but including other areas of service, such as Bible camps, week-day youth activities, films, and other areas of ministry in the general field of Christian Education. Even the Free Church Youth Fellowship, which had its own special sphere of service since its organization in 1941, has been made a part of the Christian Education department, even though it still has its own FCYF board and special projects.

Until 1953 our national Evangelical Free Church of America did not even have a Sunday School Board. There was a Sunday School Committee that had functioned in a limited way up to that time, but it did not attain board status until 1953. The first action taken by the elected Sunday School Board was to engage a man to head an official Sunday School department at our EFCA headquarters.

The choice fell to the Rev. C. Chester Larson whose considerable experience as a pastor along with a burning zeal for the promotion of Christian work among the young, made him a logical candidate for this important post. He served as Acting Secretary of the Sunday School board until 1954, when he was elected for his first three-year term as executive secretary of Sunday school work.

His enthusiasm, dedication and hard work gave a powerful impetus to the Sunday school work in our churches. He promoted the work with vigor, conducting conferences and workshops, teacher training institutes, striving to raise the standards of our Sunday school work. He succeeded in getting a large percentage of our schools to adopt a well-planned "Standard" by which to measure the success of a Sunday school.

His report to the Diamond Jubilee conference in 1959 indicated that there were more than 60,000 students enrolled in our Free Church Sunday schools at that time and about 7,000 workers. He set a goal at that time of 75,000 students and 8,500 teachers and workers to be reached by 1963.

He promoted the annual S.I.D. program (Sunday School Improvement Days), a program which reached more schools each year. He was in close touch with the National Sunday School Association, the Evangelical Teacher Training Association, and the Sunday School publishing houses, such as Gospel Light Press and Scripture Press. He promoted a special program of imprinting Gospel Light Press material with the name of the Evangelical Free Church, thus giving official approval to the material published by them and sold through the Beacon Book Store. He worked hard to implement what he called a "Program of Excellence," which urged our schools to promote "a program of *evaluation*, a program of *enlargement*, a program of *extension*, a program of *evangelism*, a program of *education*, a program of *edification*, and a program of *economy*," constantly keeping before our leaders the importance of *Building Bigger and Better Sunday Schools*.

The Sunday School department sponsored the "Read It Through in '62" program, as well as "Once More in '64." In 1963 the department urged our schools to aim at *doubling their numbers in a decade*, which would mean that by 1973 we would have 1,000 schools, 15,000 staff members, and 150,000 enrolled students in our Sunday schools.

Even as early as 1959 Mr. Larson recognized the need of establishing a Christian Education department and was looking forward to such a change in the nature of the youth program in our churches.

Mr. Larson presented his eleventh and last report to the conference in 1964. Previous to that he had met with the Sunday School Board and the board of the EFCA and the newly elected Board of Christian Education and helped to plan for the reorganization of the department with its goal of promoting "a total program of Christian education" in the Evangelical Free Church of America.

Reports to the 1965 and 1966 conferences were given by the chairman of the Board of Christian Education. The board had met many times to plan and perfect the organization of the Christian Education department and to consider whom they might recommend to succeed Mr. Larson.

After careful and prayerful consideration of the qualifications they were looking for to head the department they nominated the Rev. Kenneth Meyer, the aggressive and successful pastor of the Crystal Evangelical Free Church of Minneapolis. Mr. Meyer commenced his work as of January 1, 1967, as Acting Secretary for Christian Education until conference time, when he was elected for a three-year term for his office.

Mr. Meyer's first annual report emphasized the importance of continued effort in the building of bigger and better Sunday schools. The annual Sunday School Improvement Days program had made a greater impact than ever in providing inspiration and practical help. The board had operated in the five areas of service, with a committee cooperating in each area; namely, Sunday schools, Bible camps, week-day clubs and activities, Beacon Films, and the F.C.Y.F.

More than 8,000 boys and girls had attended Bible camps during the past year, and the film service had been greatly enlarged. The FCYF had for its program "Project Luke," which financed the coming of Luke Saba to our country from the Congo. The department was working on a plan whereby a team of young people would give ten months of their time in a sacrificial service in visitation, canvassing and evangelism.

The 1968 conference report indicated progress in the expanded ministry of the department, with a growth of 3.6% in the Sunday schools, the adoption of a new "Standard" for measuring progress, and the sponsoring of another Bible-reading program called "Every Line in '69." Leadership conferences had been held. Dr. Edwin Groenhoff was helping as a youth consultant, and they had adopted a special project for 1968-69, "Wheels for TJC," to purchase a pick-up truck for Trinity Junior College.

The Christian Education department had operated with a considerable deficit for a number of years, so that in 1964 the accumulated deficit was approximately $29,000. By 1968 this had been reduced to $8,500. Mr. Meyer reported that the income for 1967-68 was twice that of any previous year and the largest in the history of the department, which is now operating with a balanced annual budget.

As the Christian Education Board pondered how they might increase the effectiveness of their program, they came up with the idea of a Family Life Commission. We shall no doubt hear more about this "commission," which will be seeking to aid our adults as well as young people "in the facets of family life such as devotional literature, sex education based on biblical-moral principles, and Christian ethics."

In every way possible our Christian Education department is promoting those aspects of the Great Commission involving that great task of "teaching them to observe all things whatsoever I have commanded you," confident that as they do so they may count on the presence and guidance of Him who said, "And lo, I am with you always, even unto the end of the age."

SEVEN

STEWARDSHIP

A NEW STEWARDSHIP EMPHASIS

The New Testament admonishes us not only to be "good stewards of the grace of God"—in spreading the Good News of salvation—but wise stewards in handling the material resources which have been bestowed upon us. It is significant that a large percentage of the parables of our Lord emphasize the importance of right attitudes toward what He called "the Mammon of unrighteousness."

The per capita giving on the part of Free Church people has always been high compared to other denominational groups. We have been at the very *top* of the list of denominations in giving to foreign missions, and *near* the top in over-all contributions for all causes. Perhaps this is the reason our denomination has lagged behind many other groups in guiding and instructing our people in the handling of their money.

The past decade has witnessed a change in this attitude along with a greater awareness of the vital bearing good stewardship has on Christian life and Christian living. The setting up of the

CHRISTIAN INVESTORS FOUNDATION a decade ago and the establishment of a DEPARTMENT OF STEWARDSHIP at our Evangelical Free Church Headquarters three years ago have been the result of this new appreciation of the spiritual value of good stewardship in the handling of one's wealth, whether it be small or great.

CHRISTIAN INVESTORS FOUNDATION

Authorized by the 1958 annual conference, the Christian Investors Foundation was "open for business" when our Diamond Jubilee Conference convened in 1959. At that time President Arnold Olson announced that the Foundation had now been properly organized and incorporated and that Mr. Paul Carlson of Minneapolis had been appointed by the Board of Directors as secretary-treasurer of the Foundation. The Foundation received its first deposit, or investment, when the late Rev. Ivan Larson, then superintendent of the Christian Homes in Holdrege, Nebraska, presented to Mr. Carlson a check for $10,000 from a fund it had on hand for future expansion of the institution.

The Foundation operates pretty much like a savings and loan association, paying the current rate of interest on its deposits and using the money to make loans at a slightly higher rate. In the case of our Foundation, the loans are made to churches to enable them to build new edifices or to improve their facilities in other ways. In appealing to our people to invest in the Foundation, Mr. Carlson likes to suggest, "Make your money serve two masters—God and you."

Within eight months from the time the Foundation had "opened for business," more than $200,000 had been placed in the fund and the first loan had been made—a loan of $25,000 to the Evangelical Free Church of Salt Lake City, Utah, which had been unable to obtain such a loan locally. This enabled the church to complete its new sanctuary.

Deposits from Free Church people in the Foundation have increased year by year. By May 31, 1961, more than half a million dollars had been invested and 13 churches had been helped with loans. Two years later deposits passed the million mark.

By the end of December, 1968, Certificates of Deposit aggregating $2,053,700 had been issued to depositors. Including a reserve of $50,325.57, total assets of the Foundation were $2,104,025.57. Loans had been made to 75 churches, several of which had been helped more than once.

The Foundation is well managed, with its office at Free Church Headquarters, in Minneapolis, under the guidance of a Board of Directors consisting of well-known and highly respected Free Church laymen.

A DEPARTMENT OF STEWARDSHIP

Throughout the past ten years there has been a growing feeling on the part of President Arnold Olson and other leaders that a Department of Stewardship should be established to serve the entire denomination and its institutions. There had been occasional reminders, now and then, through *The Evangelical Beacon,* of the importance of making wills and of remembering the Evangelical Free Church of America by investing in annuity contracts. More and more, however, it was recognized that our EFCA needed a full-time man to direct a systematic approach to the whole field of estate planning, annuities, wills, deferred giving programs, life income agreements, etc.

At long last the right full-time man became available to head the new Department of Stewardship. Announcement was made in the August 20, 1966 issue of *The Evangelical Beacon* that the Rev. Darrel D. Stark, member of one of our churches who had served in the stewardship field for a nationally known missionary organization for ten years, would take over these responsibilities for the Evangelical Free Church on September 1, 1966. He would serve on an interim basis until conference time in 1967 when he would be nominated for a full term of three years as Secretary of Stewardship.

When Mr. Stark presented his first report, after eight months on the job, at our 1967 conference, he was already able to report that there had been an increase of $170,000 in the EFCA annuity program through his efforts. He had presented his stewardship program at District conferences, had followed up numerous requests for personal counseling in the matter of wills, annuities, estate planning, etc. He had made available to our constituency two excellent booklets—"Receiving While Giving," and "The Making of a Christian Will."

At our 1968 conference Mr. Stark reported, "Our people are becoming increasingly concerned about their plans for the ultimate disposition of the material possessions entrusted to them by the Lord." He was anticipating "increased use of estate planning seminars throughout the country." Another $117,778.48 had been added to the Annuity and Life Income program during the year, as well as $141,050 in various other types of stewardship plans In the nine months of the current fiscal year (to March 8, 1969), another $12,000 has been added to the Annuity income, $92,000 to the Life Income Plans, and $83,750 to various revocable plans.

A regular column in *The Evangelical Beacon* is conducted by Mr. Stark, who calls attention to various ways in which Christian people can take advantage of tax savings and other benefits while at the same time making possible an expansion of the Lord's work in home and foreign fields through wise stewardship with respect to their possessions.

EIGHT

TRINITY

TRINITY'S DECADE OF PROGRESS

The successful Program of Progress that reached its climax in the Diamond Jubilee Year of the Evangelical Free Church affected all phases of the work. New life and challenge were injected into the home and foreign missionary projects sponsored by the denomination. The Sunday School department had chosen for its theme and slogan, "Reaching forth unto those things which are before." The Publication department had expanded its facilities and in its concern for more space was pressing for the erection of a new headquarters and publication building that would be adequate for both present needs and future expansion.

Two decisions of our Diamond Jubilee Conference were destined to make possible the phenomenal "Decade of Progress" which has been experienced by Trinity College and Trinity Evangelical Divinity School. One of these was the proposal to increase the size of the Board of Education from nine to 21 members. Explaining the need for a larger board, the chairman reported, "Because of the limited number of members on the board, it becomes necessary for some to serve on more than one committee . . . We are convinced from past experience and also from learning the size of other boards of education representing schools of comparable size, that we should have a larger board if we are to function efficiently and smoothly."

A proposed change in the constitution to this effect was voted by the conference.

A more momentous decision had to do with the location of the Chicago school. A planning committee had been convinced that the kind of college and seminary needed by the Evangelical Free Church could not be attained at the Chicago site, in a strictly residential area. The old residences that had been acquired to house the students were entirely inadequate, and the old 4211 building and the brick structure erected in 1950 and 1951 would permit no expansion of classroom or library facilities.

The planning committee had been exploring locations north of Chicago as possible sites for the development of an adequate campus. They were not sure when they came to the conference in June of 1959 of any particular site they would recommend. They did come with a resolution, however, that gave the board freedom to consider a new location. After considerable debate, this historic resolution was finally passed, namely, "Resolved that the Board of Trustees be authorized to purchase or sell land and property adjacent to or *not* adjacent to the present location, and in addition be authorized to borrow funds needed temporarily to complete or assure the acquisition of suitable property until the 1960 conference." Questions put to the members of the board were apparently answered to the satisfaction of the conference, so that, according to the minutes, "The motion was unanimously adopted."

The decision was a victory for the planning committee of the board, which, according to Trinity's president, was "dreaming and planning for Trinity's tomorrow."

The success of the Jubilee Fund campaign enouraged the board of education to "think big" with respect to the future of Trinity.

College enrollment had reached an all-time high, taxing the limited facilities in the Chicago location to the limit. Faculty and staff were pressing for better facilities that would enable them to add new departments and courses which they considered indispensable to the development of a four-year liberal arts college. The seminary enrollment had fallen off somewhat, but Dean Douglas Young was inaugurating a new program "with particular stress on balancing the practical skills of the pastor in his parish with the great need to develop every intellectual and spiritual gif' i the student."

It must be admitted that our Evangelical Free Church constituency ten years ago had not yet been convinced of the importance of maintaining and developing a four-year liberal arts college. Up to this time there had never been a decision of our general conference to have more than a two-year college department in connection with our Bible Institute and Seminary. As a matter of fact, it was more or less of a surprise to many of our people to learn that a four-year college was being developed, step by step, by adding new courses and new faculty members to the college department of our school, even before there had been conference approval for such a development.

Conference approval was finally given to the four-year liberal arts program at the 1960 conference, at Green Lake, Wisconsin, after a historic debate that dissolved the doubts.

Dr. Franklin Olson presented the report of the joint building and planning committee of the board, which contained a resolution that would authorize the board of education to "maintain and strengthen the program of Trinity Seminary *and also to operate a four-year college.*" Before the resolution was brought to the floor of the conference it was thoroughly discussed and debated, pro and con, for a period of eight hours in a meeting of the board of directors (consisting of members of all administrative boards of the Evangelical Free Church). To begin with, it seemed that the board was almost evenly divided as to whether our Evangelical Free Church was ready to develop and maintain a four-year liberal arts college. There was strong sentiment for a junior college department at our Bible Institute and Seminary. It was feared by many that our people were not thoroughly convinced that we needed or could afford the kind of college our board of education envisioned.

Gradually the doubts were cleared away as the president and the deans answered the many questions put to them. One of the board members (not a member of the school board) commented on this eight-hour debate in this way:

> Frequently we were in need of information and explanations from our president, Dr. H. Wilbert Norton, and also from Dean Gunnar Urang. I want to say that the way these men conducted themselves, with poise and grace, and the way they answered the many questions directed to them, factually and honestly; the way they weathered the natural pressure involved without a moment of emotional or spiritual weakness evident, makes me proud of them and the fact that we have men of such quality at the helm at Trinity. I believe great days are ahead for our college and seminary under their leadership.

With a favorable recommendation from the board of directors, the resolution was brought to the conference the following day. Ample time was allowed for questions, as well as for opinions. About forty of the delegates voiced their opinions or asked questions during a three-and-one-half-hour session! At one time, Editor Mel Larson counted 623 people in the conference hall "as visitors also sat in on the interesting and important debate."

There was deep concern as to the *cost* of establishing and maintaining a college on a new campus. The resolution called for the construction of Phase I (over a four-year period from 1960 to 1964) to take place when 60 per cent (exclusive of borrowed funds) of the total cost (estimated at $2,353,000) was on hand or available. Realizing how difficult it is to raise money to pay large sums of indebtedness, the conference insisted that 70 per cent of the total cost must be on hand before beginning the construction program.

When the vote was finally taken, at 4:48 that afternoon, the vote was almost unanimous, with only two delegates standing in opposition.

The resolution approved the re-location on a 79-acre piece of property at Bannockburn, a very strategic spot at the junction of Half Day Road (Highway 22) and the Tri-State Tollway (#94), thirty miles north of downtown Chicago. Our board of education and board of trustees had negotiated a very favorable purchase from Mr. Richard E. Welch. The mansion and other buildings on the estate would enable the seminary to re-locate there the following year.

Separate corporations were formed at this time, to operate under the laws of the State of Illinois, known as Trinity College, and Trinity Theological Seminary. Up to this time there had been *one* school with its two departments or divisions. Now there would be two separate schools, yet united under one administration. The word "Bible" was eliminated from the name of the college, the explanation for which satisfied the delegates when they were assured that there would be no less Bible taught in the college and that accreditation was being sought not as a Bible college but as a liberal arts college.

Three years later, when the theological seminary was reorganized, its name was changed to Trinity Evangelical Divinity School.

There was never any question as to the importance our constituency attached to our theological seminary. The resolution authorizing the four-year college also included the purpose to "maintain and strengthen the program of Trinity Seminary."

Our 1962 conference, at Winona Lake, Indiana, instructed the board of education and the Trinity Advancement committee to "give *top priority* to the seminary in their planning." A recommendation had also been received from the Ministerial Association of Southern California, urging "a new program whose main thrust shall be geared to the establishment of a strong theological seminary at Bannockburn." This was referred to the board of education for consideration.

There were many meetings of the board of education following the 1962 conference with a view to carrying out the wishes of the conference with respect to Trinity Evangelical Divinity School. A special motion was passed at the 1963 conference commending Dr. Olson, Dr. Norton and the board of education "for the daring way in which they had carried out the instructions of last year's conference."

The "daring" decisions, approved by the 1963 conference, included the appointment of Dr. Kenneth S. Kantzer, chairman of the division of Biblical education and apologetics at Wheaton College, as dean of the Divinity school, with authority to select a faculty of outstanding evangelical scholars. Dr. G. Douglas Young had resigned as dean, desiring to devote more of his time to the American Institute of Holy Land Studies, which he had established in Jerusalem.

A few days following our 1963 conference, Dr. Norton, Trinity's president, and the Rev. Harry Evans, chairman of the board, announced that Dr. Kantzer had already completed negotiations for the following men to join the staff of the Divinity School: Dr. Wilbur M. Smith, professor of English Bible at Fuller Theological Seminary and editor of Peloubet's Select Notes on the International Sunday School Lesson; Mr. Walter Liefeld, soon to complete work for his Ph.D. at Columbia University and formerly on the staff of the Biblical Seminary of New York; Dr. Arthur Holmes of Wheaton, and Dr. Richard N. Longenecker, on leave from Wheaton College.

Two 12-unit apartment buildings for seminary married students were also authorized by the conference, construction to commence in the fall and to be completed by the fall of 1964.

This was the beginning of a new era for the theological training center of our Evangelical Free Church. Since then it has grown rapidly and gradually come to be recognized in evangelical circles as one of the outstanding theological seminaries in the country. Enrollment was only 42 in 1961-62. By the fall of 1962 a total of 66 students were enrolled. Enrollment was up to 100 in the fall of 1964 and by the fall of 1965 enrollment had increased to 229, including "institute" students (those who came for Tuesday classes only). In the fall of 1966 there were 267 full-time students, 32 part-time or special students, and another 75 who were auditing one or more courses, especially in the evening school. A year later, in the fall of 1967, the full-time student enrollment had zoomed to 325, and it had been necessary to defer the acceptance of many who wanted to come. These students came from 33 states and from nine foreign countries. Fifty-nine had Evangelical Free Church backgrounds.

An effort was being made to limit enrollment to slightly over 300, but the 1968 enrollment figure showed 338 fulltime students!

Even a brief examination of the 1968-1969 bulletin of the Divinity School will reveal the secret of the phenomenal growth of the school. Without question it is the outstanding evangelical scholars on the faculty that are attracting young men (and a few young women) from all over the country and many foreign countries. The bulletin lists 18 full-time professors, several part-time professors, ten visiting professors and four visiting lecturers. Most of these men have earned doctorates and are well known as outstanding evangelical scholars and authors of theological books.

Just as the faculty represents several different denominational backgrounds, it is understandable that the students have come from various denominations, as well as from independent churches. Seventy-five of the students who enrolled in the fall of 1968 came from Evangelical Free churches. (This figure represents the largest number of Free Church men ever to enroll in our seminary.) Students have come from several different Baptist groups, from the Christian and Missionary Alliance, from Plymouth Brethren assemblies, from Presbyterian, Covenant, and Pentecostal groups, and a considerable number from Bible churches and non-denominational groups.

Not so few of the men from other denominational backgrounds, after their three years in the Divinity school, have identified themselves with the Evangelical Free Church and accepted calls to Free Church pastorates or for foreign missionary service.

A considerable number of students attending our Divinity school are preparing for teaching careers in Bible institutes and colleges in this country or in overseas fields. After earning their M.A. or Th.M. degrees, many go on for their doctorates and then enter the teaching profession.

The growth of Trinity College has also been quite spectacular since the college moved to the new Bannockburn campus. During the first half of the decade enrollment did not vary much, running between 220 and 260. The college was sharing the very limited space and facilities with the seminary and there was neither the incentive nor the opportunity for the administration and faculty to realize the dreams they had for the college. Conference approval had been given for the development of the four-year college, and plans were being made for the occupation of the new campus at Bannockburn, but in the meantime the outward growth of the college was pretty much at a standstill, even while the leaders prepared for the day when it would be possible to move to Bannockburn.

Moving to the new campus took place in the fall of 1965, by which time a dormitory building, a food services building and an academic building (classrooms, library and offices) were ready for occupancy. These were dedicated during the week-end when Trinity's new president, the Rev. Harry L. Evans, was inaugurated and assumed his new position.

From then on the growth of the college has been spectacular. A forty percent increase in enrollment took place the first school year at the new location when 308 students were registered. A still greater increase was reported the following year when 402 students enrolled. During the school year of 1967-68 the enrollment was a little under 600, and during the 1968-69 school year it was up to almost 700. There is reason to believe that it might be up to 800 by the fall of 1969.

While the move to Bannockburn was no doubt the principal reason for the rapid growth of the college since 1965, other factors influenced the development of the school. The new president, working with the new dean, Dr. Edward Neteland, had succeeded in building a much larger faculty of fully qualified and dedicated men and women, many of them with doctors' degrees in their particular fields.

As the student body and faculty have increased, it has been necessary, of course, to add to the facilities of the college. By January of 1967 the new gymnasium-auditorium was completed which provided an adequate (though not ideal) place for the daily chapel services as well as for the athletic program of the college.

Latest building to be completed on the college side of the campus is the beautiful J. R. Johnson Residence Hall, ready for occupancy in January of 1968 and dedicated during the general conference of the Evangelical Free Church of America in June of 1968. The dormitory accommodates 232 young women students.

A still further reason for the rapid growth of the college is the fact that—especially since moving to the new campus—the college has become separate and distinct from the Divinity school, except that it has the same president and business manager and accounting department. The accrediting agency which granted full accreditation on March 26, 1968 would like to see an even greater separation from the Divinity School. Perhaps that will be another stage in the development of the college.

Our board of education and the trustee board of the Evangelical Free Church have always been concerned about the high cost of maintaining our educational institutions, and the difficulty of balancing "budgets." Year after year it was necessary for Trinity to report substantial deficits in the operation of the school. The accumulated deficit in 1960 was $39,288. By 1965 it has risen to $227,149.

The Trinity Advancement Committee (TAC) launched a drive in 1961 to raise $3,000,000 for the building program on the new campus. It proved to be a costly campaign and a great deal of effort was put into it by dedicated leaders of our school board, but somehow it did not produce the hoped-for results. In 1963 the committee reported that only five percent of the full membership of the Evangelical Free Church of America had participated in the drive and only 22 percent of the churches had responded. Total cash and pledges by the time the committee was dissolved in 1965 amounted to $688,000.

Our schools faced a financial crisis at the beginning of 1964. In addition to the accumulated deficit of more than $200,000, it appeared that an additional deficit of $150,000 would be incurred by the end of the fiscal year unless there was some way to avoid it. At the request of the board and representing a small committee of the board, the Rev. Andrew Johnson, moderator of our Free Church conference that year, issued an urgent, almost desperate, appeal covering almost two pages of *The Evangelical Beacon,* calling attention to the situation and asking for a response from every Free Church member. He wrote, "According to anticipated income and expenditures, there will be no funds available for us to operate our schools after April 1, 1964."

The response to the S.O.S. (Save Our Schools) appeal was reported to our conference in June. In three and one-half months the school received more money for operating the schools than it had in all 12 months of the previous year, approximately $100,000. The committee, however, made it clear that another $100,000 would be needed to balance the budget by August 31, and appealed to our churches for continued and increased support for the schools, urging at least $10 per member from each of our churches.

President Arnold Olson and members of the trustee board had expressed concern over the deficits and increased indebtedness incurred both through the operation of the schools and through the building program. President Olson said in his report at the 1965 conference, "Whereas this conference once expressed itself as requiring an amount not less than 70 percent of the total cost to be on hand or available before entering upon the building program, we have gradually yielded until now we have nothing on hand as we begin a building project."

Nevertheless the building program has continued and the operational costs continue to climb, and the amazing thing to report is that the unrestricted giving to our schools has increased year by year from $79,596 as of May 31, 1963 to $301,000 as of May 31, 1968, and—as if by a miracle—President Evans has been able to report that the operating budget has been raised during each of the past four years!

At our 1966 conference the board of trustees proposed a capital funds drive for $2,500,000, to be apportioned as follows: $1,500,000 for Trinity, $350,000 for Trinity Junior College, and $265,000 for the liquidation of the debt on the Headquarters building in Minneapolis. By conference time a year later the campaign (United Development Crusade) was ready to be launched. The goal, however, was subsequently boosted to $3,250,000, with the provision that the churches participating in the campaign would be permitted to retain 25 percent of the amount raised for their own local program. The remaining sum would be apportioned as follows: Headquarters 12.5 percent, Trinity Junior College 16.5 percent, and Trinity College and Trinity Evangelical Divinity School 71 percent.

Dr. Henry Nelson, Director of the United Development Crusade (U.D.C.), reported in the December 31, 1968 issue of the Beacon that as of that time approximately 70 churches had pledged more than $500,000 and that another 70 churches had indicated that they would participate in the campaign. It doesn't take much figuring to see that *if* the 70 churches which have agreed to participate do as well as the 70 churches that have completed their campaigns, and another 300 churches participate and do as well, the goal will be reached.

The question of seeking Federal aid to help finance the construction of college buildings was raised among members of the board of education. Other colleges were receiving large grants from the government for this purpose, and some of our school men were asking, Why should Trinity turn down such a golden opportunity?

This was the crucial question confronting our general conference in 1966. The question, however, had been raised the previous year, at which time the Committee for Safeguarding Our Spiritual Heritage had been asked to study the matter and report its findings to the 1966 conference. The committee was unanimous in recommending that Federal grants be turned down. The board of education was divided on the subject and came to the conference with both a majority and a minority report, the majority report favoring the acceptance of grants. Thinking there was the *possibility* of conference approval, the college had in the meantime made application for a grant and had been assured of the sum of $183,000 to help build a much-needed science building.

After a thorough discussion of the matter by the board of directors of the conference, its recommendation to postpone final action on the question for one year was voted by the conference. A new committee was selected to secure more information that might guide the delegates in their vote at the 1967 conference.

Members of the committee took their assignment seriously and studied the question thoroughly and conscientiously, reporting their findings in special articles in the denominational magazine. Coming to the conference at Long Beach, Calif. in 1967, the recommendation of the Committee on Safeguarding Our Spiritual Heritage was given unanimous approval by the conference after the inclusion of three little words in the paragraph. The resolution, with the three added words in italics, is as follows:

After much prayer and careful study of all phases of this important question, we as participating members of the committee have come to the unanimous conclusion that the Evangelical Free Church of America should not *at this time* ask or accept Federal grants to its institutions for the following reasons, which are also supported by the documents accompanying this report.

A subsequent motion was passed which approved the acceptance of long-term *loans* as far as they relate to dormitories.

The conviction that God would supply the means for the advancement of His work, through His own people, was strengthened by a very happy announcement at this conference, namely, that "an anonymous donor has contributed 6,000 shares of stock worth about $150,000 to the Divinity school for a library building."

Subsequent gifts from the same source (not a member of the Evangelical Free Church) have increased this fund to almost $360,000, which has encouraged the administration to proceed with the construction of a $700,000 Divinity school library as soon as possible. By conference time in 1969 it will be reported that the library building, including a lecture hall and some offices, is actually under construction.

Ground-breaking for the new library, to be called the James E. Rolfing Memorial Library—took place on Sunday afternoon, April 27, 1969, with Dr. Wilbur M. Smith as principal speaker for the occasion.

A further indication of the confidence people outside the Evangelical Free Church have in the work of our educational institutions is a recent grant by the W. Clement and Jessie V. Stone Foundation of Chicago of $45,000 to develop an "Achievement Motivation Program" in the college. This project was introduced officially on October 3, 1968, when Mr. Stone addressed a convocation on the campus and presented each student and faculty member present a package of books designed to inspire young people to put their very best effort into their work.

Before leaving the subject of financing for our schools, it

should be reported that, at about the same time a denominational stewardship secretary was engaged for the Minneapolis office, Trinity College and Trinity Evangelical Divinity School engaged a former building contractor from California, Mr. David Wennstrom, as a development officer, to conduct "a continuing stewardship program." He took courses to prepare him for this work and worked hard, according to President Harry Evans' report to the 1967 conference, "cultivating across the country a nucleus of interested and influential friends of Trinity." He offers guidance in "setting one's house in order" to make sure that one's wishes will be carried out after his decease. He is a firm believer in and offers advice in "estate planning" to avoid unnecessary waste in the handling and distribution of one's assets. His efforts are producing dividends that will accrue to the benefit of the Lord's work and Trinity in the years to come.

Changes in administrative posts have influenced the progress of Trinity during the past decade. With the resignation of Mr. Gunnar Urang as Dean of Trinity College, in 1961, it was necessary to secure a man of comparable stature to take over the administration of the college. President Norton introduced the new dean at our 1961 conference, namely Dr. Lacy Hall, who had been dean of students at King's College and had earned his doctor's degree in education at Columbia University. Dr. Hall responded by saying, in part, "I have received my assignment to get Trinity College fully accredited."

A good start was made during Dr. Hall's term toward the accrediting of the college. In 1964, however, he gave up his connection with the college and joined the faculty of the Divinity school, at which time Dr. Edward Neteland, who also had a doctorate in the field of education, took over, first as acting dean and later as dean of the college. Dr. Neteland had been serving as assistant dean and chairman of the department of education during the previous year. He was reared in the Salem Free Church of Chicago and is an active member of that congregation.

Dr. Neteland continued the endeavor of the college to attain full accreditation by the North Central Association. He was concerned with raising the educational standards of the college in order to achieve this goal. For six years the college had been striving to attain this accreditation. For three years they worked on a "self-study" that enabled them to achieve "candidate status." During the past three years Dr. Neteland and his team redoubled their efforts to meet the requirements which the examining board had suggested. They approached the last week of March of 1969 with a mixture of confidence and apprehension, knowing they would get either good news or bad when the North Central Association had its meeting at that time.

The news was imparted to President Evans, Dr. Henry Nelson and Dr. Robert Hansen on Wednesday morning, March 26, and it was the best news that could possibly be heard—ACCREDITATION HAD BEEN APPROVED!

The event was celebrated with a jubilant convocation in the college gymnasium on Thursday morning, March 27, at which time the administration, faculty and student body congratulated each other and themselves, and offered thanks to God for the attainment of this goal that had been sought with such hard work over the past six years.

Dr. Neteland has done such an effective job in his position as dean of the college that he has now been promoted to the newly created office of vice president for institutional advancement. His new responsibilities "will have their outreach to the various publics of both schools, to enhance their position, stability and purposes," according to President Evans.

Replacing Dr. Neteland as dean of the college will be Dr. J. Edward Hakes, who has been chairman of the division of Christian education of the Divinity school. His title will be vice president for undergraduate studies and dean of the college.

Dr. Hakes is the former president of the Grand Rapids Baptist Seminary and former assistant professor of Bible at Wheaton College. He has pastored several churches and is the author of

Introduction to Evangelical Christian Education (Moody Press).

In announcing the recommendation of Dr. Hakes by the board of education, President Evans also announced the resignation of the Rev. R. Dean Smith, who leaves in August to become superintendent of the Great Lakes District Association. Mr. Smith has been executive secretary of the Alumni Association, director of public relations, and director of development.

Announcement was also made that Dr. Kenneth Kantzer, dean of the seminary, will also be vice president for graduate studies, and Mr. Phil Gustafson, who has carried the title of business manager, will become vice president for business affairs.

The most significant change in the administration of our Bannockburn schools came following the resignation of Dr. H. Wilbert Norton, in 1964. The former missionary in our Congo field had been teaching at Trinity for several years. A highlight of our 1957 conference was the installation of Dr. Norton as president of the college and seminary on Thursday night of the conference. Dr. Norton's leadership in the development of our schools, and very especially in guiding the re-location to the new campus, was recognized in a resolution passed by the 1964 conference, which read in part:

> We commend Dr. H. Wilbert Norton for his tireless dedication to his work at Trinity these past 14 years, and for his dedication to the cause of Jesus Christ and the Evangelical Free Church of America over the past 25 years.

The resolution expressed the desire for his "continued service" in the coming years.

Dr. David R. Anderson, vice president of Trinity, served as acting president for some months following Dr. Norton's departure until March, 1965, when the board of education appointed the Rev. Harry L. Evans executive vice president for the remainder of the school year, thereafter to serve as acting president as of June 5. Mr. Evans had been chairman of the board during the previous four years and was intimately familiar with all phases of school affairs. The board felt that his administrative ability and excellent rapport with our Free Church constituency fully qualified him to assume this position. Brought up in the Evangelical Free Church, he had served churches in Brooklyn, New York; Gothenburg, Nebraska, and for the past six and one-half years at Arlington Heights, Illinois.

An important item of business of the 1965 conference was the election of Mr. Evans as president of our schools at Bannockburn. At age 35 he had already proven himself a capable administrator. Even before his election he had been busy during the preceding months directing a program to balance the budget by August 31 (end of the fiscal year). It was good news to our entire constituency when his announcemenet appeared in the September 28 issue of *The Evangelical Beacon* reading:

> We are pleased to be able to announce that due to the generosity of our churches and individuals who have a deep interest in Trinity, our budget has been balanced as of August 31, 1965, for this fiscal year.

Similar announcements were made by President Evans in the fall of 1966, again in 1967, and in the fall of 1968. After so many years of operating our schools with deficits, there was rejoicing at the reversal of that trend.

And no one will question the fact that Harry Evans deserves more credit than he himself claims for this outstanding achievement.

The inauguration of the new president took place at a most impressive convocation service, held in the Deerfield high school auditorium on Sunday, November 21, 1965, with Dr. Walter H. Judd as the guest speaker for the occasion. College buildings completed that fall, making possible the move from Chicago to the new campus, were dedicated on the same weekend, on Saturday the 20th.

Taking part in the inauguration program were Dr. Arnold

Olson, president of the Evangelical Free Church of America, Dr. David H. Johnson, general director emeritus of TEAM, and the architects and contractors involved in the building program. Also taking part was Dr. C. Raymond Gibson, Trinity's academic consultant and chairman of the department of higher education at Indiana University. Dr. Judd's message pointed out the responsibility of the Christian college in producing Christian leadership "to guard our heritage of freedom which is gravely threatened by a cold, determined assault from without and by ignorance and apathy within."

Following the 1968 conference, in June, President Evans, with the help of landscape architects and campus planners, presented the ten-year master plan for Trinity's development to the Village of Bannockburn. The goal as visualized for the next few years, according to President Evans, is as follows: On the college side, a college classroom addition, a science building, a library, another dormitory, student union, and a chapel-auditorium. On the Divinity school side, a classroom-office building, a library, a chapel, and a student union, as well as whatever additional housing may be essential.

The 70th anniversary of the establishment of Trinity, back in 1897, was observed in October of 1967. A brief sketch of Trinity's history appeared in a special issue of the *Beacon* together with pictures of classes from as far back as the first class of 1897. The anniversary concert more than filled the spacious gymnasium-auditorium with its capacity of more than 2,000 people. Almost 1,100 friends of Trinity partook of the buffet dinner served in the dining hall preceding the concert, at which time George Beverly Shea (whose son was a student at Trinity) thrilled the audience with his presentation of the Gospel in song.

Now Trinity is looking forward to its 75th anniversary, in 1972, and tentative plans are already being made for a worthy observance of this Diamond Jubilee.

NINE

TRINITY JUNIOR

A JUNIOR COLLEGE IN CANADA "IN ORBIT"

The decade following the merger of the two Evangelical Free Church groups witnessed considerable growth in both the number and the strength of the Evangelical Free churches in the Prairie provinces and British Columbia, in Canada. By the first of January, 1959, there were nearly 70 churches in these districts that were part of the Evangelical Free Church fellowship.

There are many Bible institutes in these Canadian provinces and these have attracted hundreds of Free Church young people from our missionary-minded churches in Canada; but Christian liberal arts colleges have been practically non-existent, which means that young people desiring a liberal arts education have had no place to go except to the secular colleges and universities.

This is the situation that prompted leaders in our Canadian churches to begin to pray for and to work for the establishment of a Christian liberal arts Junior College in their country.

As early as 1956 the idea of a Junior College on the west coast, preferably in Canada, was first introduced at a meeting of the board of directors at an annual conference. Purpose of the school would be "to give young people the first two years of a university training, after which the students can pursue their specialized training in some other institution; also to provide guidance for young people as they seek direction for their lives and to train specialists for the mission fields (such as technicians, teachers, medical workers, etc.), and to provide 'Trinity training' closer to home."

Two years later a delegation of ministers and laymen from our churches in Canada came to the 1958 conference at Winona Lake, Indiana, to support a resolution that had been drafted by a committee of the Free Church board of education together with two of the Canadian leaders, which presented the need of a junior college and requested a small appropriation to explore the possibilities of establishing such a school.

The "exploratory committee," consisting of President Will Norton and representatives from the Canadian districts and from the Pacific Northwest District, met several times during subsequent months, making a careful survey of both the need and the possibilities of such a project. They came to the conference in 1959 with recommendations that a two-year (junior) college be established in the lower mainland of British Columbia and that Jubilee Program of Progress funds subscribed in Canada be allocated to secure the necessary property to begin such a school; also that a joint committee be appointed to take initial steps to implement the project.

Dr. Arnold Olson kept our constituency fully informed as each step was taken in the creation and development of the school. By April of 1960 it was possible to reproduce on the cover page of *The Evangelical Beacon* a picture of a 115-acre farm located near Langley, B. C., close to where the projected Trans-Canada Highway would come. Dr. Olson considered "one of the most eventful and significant months in Free Church history" was January of that year when the purchase of the Bannockburn property was made as well as an option taken on the purchase of the future campus for Trinity Junior College.

Later in 1960 announcement was made of the purchase of the so-called "Seal-Kap farm" and that permission was being sought to erect temporary buildings on the site. Work had also started in planning permanent buildings, curriculum, personnel, etc.

In the December 27, 1960 issue of *The Evangelical Beacon* Dr. Olson included the approval of plans for the new junior college as one of the "top events" of the year, especially since the new school would be the first Free Church institution in Canada. He quoted the Minister of Education of British Columbia as saying that the new school was "one of the most significant events in the history of education in the province," since this would provide a place where young people would be able to obtain their first two years of college along with a good foundation in the Scriptures, and where, "under the guidance of dedicated instructors, they might find God's direction for their lives."

It was pointed out that in all of western Canada, there was not a single Christian college at that time.

Having been authorized to proceed with the selection of the necessary teaching and administrative personnel, the school committee made its nominations. They felt they had been divinely led in their nomination of the Rev. Calvin B. Hanson as president of the school. A graduate of Trinity Seminary in 1945, he attended Wheaton College from 1945 to 1947. He received his B.A. from Augsburg College in Minneapolis and his M.A. from the University of Minnesota, where he was at the time completing his class work for a doctorate. He was the first missionary to go to Japan under the Overseas Board of the EFCA in 1949 and was one who helped to found the Bible institute there and start the radio broadcasts in Japanese. He had also served as assistant pastor of the First Evangelical Free Church of Minneapolis and interim pastor of Central Free Church of the same city.

Other men to serve with Dr. Hanson were Dr. Enoch E. Mattson, with Th.M. and Th D. degrees from Dallas Theological Seminary, as dean of education and registrar; Rev. Perry Havens, a former secretary-treasurer of Prairie Bible Institute, as vice president in charge of business administration, and Mr. Leland Asa, a graduate of Northwestern College and Trinity Seminary, as dean of students.

With the fall of 1962 set as the opening of the college, the next concern was the erection of necessary buildings. Dormitories were already under construction, as approved by the 1960 conference. A chapel-library building—a project of the Women's Missionary Society—was in the planning stage.

The ground-breaking and dedication of the 115-acre campus on October 8, 1961 was a thrilling and happy occasion, with the president of the newly created college delivering the dedicatory address and Mr. Harold P. Halleen, moderator of the Free Church conference, also taking part, as well as Dean Enoch Mattson, Rev. Perry Havens, Rev. Herbert Kyrk, Rev. Virgil Bergman, Rev. Carl Fosmark and Rev. David Enarson.

By the end of the year the three dormitories were nearing completion and construction of the chapel-library was scheduled to commence in February, for completion by the time of the opening of school in the fall.

The 24-page catalog for the 1962-63 year came off the press by the end of January, 1962. Temporary financing for the chapel-library had been arranged pending the gift from the Women's Missionary Society, which would help to pay for the building. A Founders Club had been formed to give people an opportunity to have a part in the founding of the new college.

In early summer, in order to raise money for the building program, thirty acres of the property were sold for $30,000, leaving the college with an 80-acre campus.

In making his first report to the 1962 conference, President Hanson described the experiences of those who had been charged with responsibility for the new school as "living on the raw edge of faith." He reported that the dormitories were completed, the chapel-library building was "moving ahead," and that present structures on the former farm were being adapted for offices, dining facilities, housing for faculty, and a temporary gymnasium.

President Hanson and family arrived on campus, from Minneapolis, on July 2, 1962, after six days of strenuous driving and camping on the way. While enjoying the magnificent mountain scenery on his way, he confessed to the fact that he was concerned about "the mountain of work to be done" before classes could commence in September.

September 11 marked the beginning of the orientation program as the first class gathered in the nearly-completed chapel-library building. The student body consisted of one from Illinois, one from Alberta, two from Washington, and ten from British Columbia. Three more were soon added to swell the enrollment to 17. President Hanson commented on the "high caliber of young people" which the Lord had sent to the school for this "pioneering first class." The chapel-library was filled almost to capacity for the first convocation, on September 18.

Dedication took place during the Ministerial Institute held on the new campus early in October. Dr. H. Wilbert Norton delivered an excellent message as he installed the president and faculty. Dr. Arnold Olson also took part with a fitting message—the same message, as he explained, that he had delivered at the time of the merger of the two schools that had been operated by the two Free Church groups up to the time of the merger.

A junior college in British Columbia was an innovation in 1962, so that Trinity Junior College was really "blazing a trail" at a time when "official opinion was lukewarm toward junior colleges," as Mr. Ray Stewart, then assistant supervisor of special education for the Surrey, B.C. school district, has pointed out. Since then, especially since a new president at the University of British Columbia assumed office, there has been a change of attitude and a very favorable attitude toward Trinity Junior College, whose students receive full credit when they transfer to the University.

The description of the first graduation at Trinity Junior College by the Rev. Hugh Walker reflects the historical significance of the occasion:

> In a blaze of golden splendor the sun was setting. Radiant beams flooded the green carpeted fields, pouring through the crystal glass into the place of dedication. Black-robed figures moved in quiet dignity through the rays of gold to the dais of the sanctuary. This was historic. God was uniquely present. There was a sense of miracle in the air. It was the reality of a vision brought to the place of birth and breathing life, the life of the eternal.

History was indeed in the making as the three first graduates of Trinity Junior College were handed their diplomas by President Hanson on that beautiful evening late in May of 1963.

Reporting to the 1963 conference in June, President Hanson called this first year at Trinity Junior College a year of "miracles and milestones." He was grateful to God for His blessing upon student body and faculty during this first year and was anticipating a much larger student body and an enlarged faculty and improved facilities when the new school year opened in September.

When school opened in September, with 48 students enrolled, President Hanson described the campus as "bulldozers, tractors, diggers, trucks and steamrollers swarmed over the campus to plow the river bank, scrape off the top-soil, load, transport and level it in preparation for seeding the lawn."

The year 1964 saw the erection and dedication of a science building, completed in time for use at the beginning of the fall semester at the low cost of $75,000, exclusive of furnishings. Dr. Arnold Olson, members of the trustee board of the Evangelical Free Church and local dignitaries were present and took part in the dedication service on October 17, 1964.

With 101 students enrolled at the beginning of the fall semester —a 100 percent increase over the preceding year—Dr. Arnold Olson commented that there was no question but that the college was "in orbit." He called attention to the fact that Trinity Junior

College's graduates were already being accepted in ten universities and colleges in Canada and the United States without the loss of credit.

"Miracles and milestones" continued to be experienced by President Hanson and his faithful colleagues who were still living "on the raw edge of faith" in 1965. This is the year that prayers were answered by means of a $50,000 gift for a library building. They had been encouraged to pray for a new library building through a generous gift of books from the library of Mr. Helmer Anderson of Central Free Church of Minneapolis, who, before his homegoing, had not only designated his own library for Trinity Junior College but had inspired many of his friends to donate books to this cause.

The announcement of the gift, from a Free Church family in the Middle West, was made early in the year, and ground broken for the building at a sunrise service on Easter Sunday. Construction was "well ahead of schedule" by the middle of the summer, and dedication took place on October 23. Highlights of the program were the first appearance of the college choir, pertinent sentiments of the donor conveyed by President Hanson, and the address by the Rev. Harry L. Evans, president of Trinity College and Trinity Evangelical Divinity School. The donor had requested that his sentiments be shared with the college constituency, namely, that he, though residing a great distance from TJC, had been inspired to give because of the sacrificial giving of faculty, staff, and the inner circle of TJC friends.

During the school year of 1965-66 the college received further recognition when approval was given by the British Columbia Student Aid Loan Committee for interest-free loans on the same basis as students in the provincial universities.

The summer months of 1966 were spent in preparing for the expected larger student body in the fall. An athletic director was engaged, books were added to the library, buildings and grounds were put in shipshape condition, and faculty and staff were preparing their own souls to meet the challenge of the coming year.

The fifty percent increase in enrollment they had hoped for materialized, with the announcement that the 150-mark had been reached. Five students from overseas were registered—four from Hong Kong and one from Japan.

The week-end of March 3-5, 1967 saw TJC's first Homecoming event, with the crowning of the homecoming "queen," the homecoming banquet, etc.

With the launching of the United Development Campaign it was announced that Trinity Junior College would receive a percentage of the total amount received, which would amount to $350,000 if the campaign reached its goal. This was a great encouragement to President Hanson and his colleagues.

There had been disappointments during the year. The new gymnasium-auditorium building, for which ground had been broken in March, had not materialized, and the new dormitory and dining hall, which was expected to be ready for the opening of the fall semester, was not completed so that temporary and emergency measures had to be found for accommodating the 217 students who enrolled in the fall of 1967.

When finally completed, the new dormitory and dining hall proved to be a "delight," containing a lounge with island fireplace, spacious recreational facilities, apartments for resident deans and auxiliary service units, etc.

The sixth annual graduation exercises, held on June 7, 1968, culminated in the presentation of 25 graduates for their diplomas. The program included a greeting from Dr. Wilhelm Gilbert, president of the International Federation of Free Evangelical Churches, and a challenging address from the Honorable Matthew Hill, senior judge of the Washington State Supreme Court. There was standing applause by the standing-room-only audience when Dr. Mattson read the citation and announced that TJC President Calvin Hanson had been awarded the honorary degree of Doctor of Letters by Trinity College and Trinity Evangelical Divinity School at their graduation exercises on May 31.

As of this writing Trinity Junior College is still going strong, being in the middle of its 1968-69 academic year (its seventh) with a near-capacity enrollment of over 250 young people. President Hanson commented in the *Beacon* after the beginning of the new semester, "We are grateful for the privilege of starting a brand new year with dorms all in readiness, classrooms ready and no major problems hanging over our heads . . . Student activities—musical, athletic, social—are being organized and an air of excitement is evident as we get started in a year which we confidently expect to be the best yet in every dimension."

TEN

MINISTERIAL ASSOCIATION

MINISTERIAL ASSOCIATION MOVES AHEAD

When the Evangelical Free Church of America celebrated its "big" anniversary—the Diamond Jubilee—in 1959, the Ministerial Association observed its 65th, which was not considered important enough for any extra-special celebration. This year, however, when the denomination as such comes to its 85th annual conference, the Ministerial Association is observing its Diamond Jubilee as it commemorates 75 years of association together in the preaching of the Gospel.

In observance of this event the Ministerial Association has published a book—the most ambitious project yet attempted by the Association—in which a historical sketch of the entire 75-year period has been prepared, as well as a bit of biographical material and a picture of each of the members of the Association (or as many as responded to the request for such data in time for publication).

This would seem to make it unnecessary to include any detailed history of the Association during the past decade. We are including, however, the most important events of the past ten years, as we have done for other organizations, institutions and departments of the Evangelical Free Church.

After accepting forty new members at the 65th annual conference in 1959, total membership of the Association reached the highest figure in its history—640 members (compared to 37 in 1894). The only other business of any importance at that conference was the unanimous decision to accept the Health Plan of the Ministers Life and Casualty Union presented by the board. For many years committees had studied various hospitalization plans, recognizing the need of some plan which would provide a measure of financial assistance in time of serious illness. Now the plan had been adopted by the 200 ministers present at the meeting, and other members of the association would be contacted immediately with full information about the Plan.

During subsequent years annual reports of the association have included such statements as "The health plan is functioning well. It has provided a much-needed service for all who are participating in it."

As of January 1, 1969, more than 360 ministers were members of the plan. Total membership of the ministerial association reported at our 1968 conference was 782. A careful screening of the membership following the conference, however, reduced the total membership to 760.

There has been steady and consistent growth of the Ministers Annuity and Aid Plan during the past decade. Ten years ago total assets in the fund were $272,459.70. The sum of $44 in receipts and earnings was being credited to the account of 235 members, including 29 who were over 65 years of age. Three hundred churches had contributed to the Plan, according to the report.

Nine years later, in 1968, total assets had increased to $587,-294.13 and the pro-rated sum credited to the account of each of the 449 members was $75. Realizing that the credit accruing to the account of the members was not keeping up with the increased cost of living, approval has now been given to an increase in the member's annual cost from $25 to $50. Churches, too, are being urged to contribute more than the $1.00 per member they have been paying into the fund since the plan was launched.

Ministerial "institutes" have been an annual event sponsored by the Association for many years. These have continued during the past years and have brought much inspiration, blessing and challenge to the ministers. There is a minimum of business at these conferences, which means there is a maximum of good solid Bible teaching and lectures on subjects of special interest and help to pastors, along with the best of Christian fellowship. These institutes usually attract up to 200 or more ministers, who then go back to their churches with new enthusiasm for the work of the ministry.

Members of the Association through the years have been concerned about the quality of instruction given to their young people, especially those in the so-called "confirmation" classes, or Bible instruction classes, conducted by the pastor. Catechisms have been prepared by committees or individual members of the Association which have served for the past fifty years or more. The latest of these, entitled *Essentials of the Christian Faith,* was prepared by Dr. Roy A. Thompson in cooperation with a committee of the Ministerial Association, in 1960. It contains 29 lessons in Bible doctrine plus a series of Bible passages suggested for memory work, a brief historical sketch of the Evangelical Free Church of America, the Free Church Statement of Faith, and a glossary of terms used in the book. The book has had a wide distribution, the fourth edition having been printed last year.

There has been a growing feeling, however, that a more comprehensive course of study should be made available for these Bible instruction classes, and a special committee has been working on the project for several years. The committee has made some progress in preparing the material, which will include not only Bible doctrine, but Bible history, Church history, Free Church history, Christian living, etc. Many of our pastors are eagerly waiting for the completion and publication of these books, which should increase the effectiveness of the pastor's Bible instruction classes.

During the past ten years there has been a greater awareness on the part of our ministers with respect to the social problems of our day. With respect to the civil rights issue the Association expressed itself at its 1963 conference as follows: "We pledge ourselves anew to uphold the rights of all, regardless of color. We register our opposition to discrimination and suppression, while at the same time opposing all attempts to deal with these difficult problems by violence."

It might be pointed out that a number of our churches are ministering to minority groups. A church in Brooklyn is working especially among the Spanish-speaking people. Two California churches are ministering to Chinese, and another to the Mexicans. One of our churches in Chicago is working in an inner city community where several different races and nationalities are represented.

On the subject of ecumenism, or fellowship with other groups, our Ministerial Association has expressed itself as follows: "That we continue to emphasize true Biblical unity, the unity of the 'one body' in Christ, entered only by the new birth, involving agreement on the great essentials, transcending all denominational lines and at least partially answering the prayer of our Lord, 'that they all may be one.' "

It must be said that our leaders have almost always been active in interdenominational evangelical movements and organizations. We have been affiliated with the National Association of Evangelicals almost from the beginning of that organization. At the present time the president of our denomination is the president of the Association, and the director of our Overseas Missions has recently retired as president of the Evangelical Foreign Missions Association. Our ministers, likewise, have been active in such evangelical organizations as Campus Crusade, Inter-

Varsity Christian Fellowship, Youth for Christ, the Billy Graham Evangelistic Association, the American Bible Society, the Evangelical Alliance Mission (the director of which is a member of our Association), etc.

The president of our denomination has also been active in the International Federation of Free Evangelical Churches for many years and has been instrumental in influencing the denomination to affiliate with the Federation. Dr. Olson's recent book, *Believers Only*, tells the story of the fourteen church bodies in Europe, as well as the three in North America, which are working together and enjoying the fellowship and inspiration of the conferences conducted by the International Federation of which they are a part.

Chairman Andrew E. Johnson of our Ministerial Association, in his report to our 74th annual conference, re-stated what he called "the five broad, basic principles that have characterized our fellowship from the beginning." He listed these as

(1) Absolute confidence in the Bible as the Word of God.
(2) A vital evangelistic outlook.
(3) A strong outreach in home and overseas missions.
(4) Separation from worldliness and doctrinal and moral evil and a positive commitment to deep moral and spiritual values in our everyday relationships.
(5) An intelligent, sane but vibrant emphasis relative to the coming again of our blessed Lord and Savior Jesus Christ, first for His own, before the Great Tribulation, and then a second coming to the earth to set up His kingdom.

Will the coming years witness a watering down of some of these "basic principles," such as has happened in other denominations? Can we look for a gradual shifting of emphasis from the *most* important to the *less* essential doctrines of our faith? Will the broadening of the curriculum in our college and Divinity school with its emphasis on psychology and counseling, and on modern social problems, have a tendency to weaken the convictions with respect to the necessity of the new birth, the inerrancy of the Scriptures, the literal resurrection of Christ from the dead, and the assurance of the literal, personal and premillennial coming of the Lord Jesus Christ?

If the Lord tarries another 25 years and our Association observes its centennial, we trust it will still be true that our Evangelical Free Church Ministerial Association has not faltered or deviated from "the faith once for all delivered unto the saints."

ELEVEN

WOMEN'S MISSIONARY SOCIETY

THE "ONWARD AND UPWARD" PROGRESS OF THE WOMEN'S MISSIONARY SOCIETY

Ten years after the organization of the Women's Missionary Society, the women chose the motto that has inspired them during the past half century. Observing their 60th birthday at Bannockburn last summer, while looking back and thanking God for the past, their aspirations were still "Onward and Upward."

Looking back, they recalled the first national project undertaken by the Society—the building of a missionary residence for Free Church missionaries in Canton, China. It had taken eight years to raise the $12,000 to pay for the mission home, which was an extremely big project for the infant society. After completing that project they were challenged by other needs, especially on the home front, meanwhile building up their membership and preparing for "onward and upward" programs as they faced the future.

Up to the time of the Diamond Jubilee conference of 1959, the Women's Missionary Society had completed 17 special home and foreign missionary projects. They had just gone "over the top" again in raising money for the furnishing of a girls' dormitory at Trinity, which they had purchased the previous year.

Though the growth of the Women's Missionary Society during the past decade may not be considered spectacular, it has been steady and consistent, gaining momentum as its membership and financial strength have increased from year to year. They were now prepared to undertake bigger and bigger projects in their determination to move "onward and upward."

Their most ambitious project for a one-year drive was launched ten years ago at the inspiring Diamond Jubilee conference. They set out to raise enough money for the purchase of a missionary furlough residence in Minneapolis, not too far from the national headquarters of the denomination. As was to be expected, they exceeded their goal and turned over a check for $18,000 to the Secretary of Overseas Missions at our 1960 conference, to make possible the purchase of a very suitable two-family dwelling for this purpose.

National projects continued to be over-subscribed throughout the remainder of the present decade. The need of a radio station in our Venezuela field was presented at the 1961 conference as a project worthy of the efforts of the Society. The money was raised and is being used to buy time for Gospel broadcasting on secular stations, since it was not possible to secure a permit to build the hoped-for station.

The chapel-library building for Trinity Junior College at Langley, B.C. the following year was a very popular project and there was no difficulty in raising the promised sum to help finance this project. The beautiful building which the W.M.S. helped to build is a constant reminder of the interest of the women in higher Christian education.

The following year (1963) they completed their project for the purchase of an old castle in Germany for the establishment of a Bible institute, and launched their project for 1964 for a revolving fund of $21,000 for Gospel centers in Japan, completed by conference time the following summer as usual.

Expecting that a chapel building would soon be erected on the Trinity Evangelical Divinity School campus, the Society adopted for its 1965 project the raising of funds for the furnishing of the chapel.

When the need of Gospel centers in the Philippines was presented, the Society responded by raising a revolving fund for this purpose, as they had done for Japan two years previously.

A similar need was presented at the 1966 conference for the field in Malaysia, whereupon the Society undertook, and completed, the raising of a substantial fund for the planting of new churches in Malaysia and Singapore, turning over a check for almost $20,000 for this purpose at our 1967 conference.

The biggest project to date is the one launched in 1967 and completed in 1968 for the raising of $25,000 for the purchase of books for the library of Trinity College, which was in dire need of a substantial enlargement of its library, which was one of the requirements for the accreditation the college was seeking. Going way "over the top" for this project, it was possible, during our 1968 conference at Trinity College, to turn over the biggest check the treasurer had ever written, representing the sum of $30,324.55!

The total annual income of the Society during the nine-year period from 1959 to 1968 increased from $34,559.67 in 1959 to $62,000 in 1968.

So much for the annual national projects, which have contributed so much to the over-all home and foreign missionary work of the Evangelical Free Church. It is understandable that the national projects have always received a primary interest and the bigger share of the publicity. The Society, however, has always maintained a much broader interest and ministry.

Next to the launching of the special annual projects, the Society's aim and purpose has been to continue to support the missionaries it has pledged to support on our various overseas mission fields. For many years they have supported six missionaries on the field, assuming the support of one after another. As of 1968 the missionaries receiving their support and the full moral and spiritual backing of the W.M.S. are Miss Elizabeth Anderson, Mrs. Nils Oldberg and Mrs. Byron Seashore in the Congo; Mrs. Stanley Conrad in Japan; Mrs. Al Unrau in the Philippines, and Miss Lorraine Ditmar in Venezuela.

Since 1966 they have taken on the support of still another missionary, though she must be classified as a home missionary since her field is in our 49th state of Alaska. She is Mrs. Robert Hoobyar, serving with her husband at Fairbanks.

Out of their missionary funds the women have also sent a check each year at Christmas time to each of the overseas missionaries of the Evangelical Free Church. In 1959 this check amounted to $8.50, but as funds increased, this annual Christmas gift increased from year to year until in 1968 it was $17.50. Letters from the missionaries acknowledging these gifts and expressing their warm appreciation have encouraged the women to continue this very fine practice.

Still another one of the missionary projects of the Society has been the White Cross work, a work that began on the local level through groups making articles and rolling bandages to be used by missionaries supported by them. "With nurses and doctors, dispensaries, and finally a hospital in the Congo, the work snowballed so that it became necessary to have a sort of clearing-house for information about needs and how to go about filling them." The second vice president of the WMS acts as White Cross chairman through whom the various local groups are contacted.

Nor do the women neglect the home missionary projects. The practice, begun in 1953, when the Shareholders program was initiated, has been continued throughout the past decade. The sum of $500 has been contributed to each project for 500 "shares" in helping to finance the erection of new church buildings throughout our country and Canada. With three to four Shareholders projects each year, this has involved an "investment" of from $1,500 to $2,000 each year in these projects.

The Women's Missionary Society has considered it missionary work to make an annual contribution to *The Evangelical Beacon,* not only in appreciation of the space given for the promotion of the Society's program, but to make possible an ever-increasing effectiveness of the denominational magazine. During the past few years they have added $1,000 a year to their contribution to make possible the sending of the *Beacon* to our missionaries by air-mail, so they would receive it almost as early as the subscribers in the home land.

An interesting project sponsored by the Society six years ago was the collecting and counting of 57,645 Betty Crocker coupons. The coupons made possible the acquisition of silverware for the lounge at Free Church Headquarters and the missionary furlough home in Minneapolis, and the residence and Bible institute in Germany. Last year another gathering of Betty Crocker coupons —294,000 of them—made possible the purchase of two pianos for Trinity schools at Deerfield.

For the past several years the Society has also provided a generous scholarship each year for each of our three schools. This sum is given to "the returning senior student who has proved himself, or herself, spiritually and academically outstanding, who may be in financial need, and who feels directed into full-time service on the home or overseas fields."

The Society has also contributed to special home missions projects during the past four years. During 1965 and 1966 their gift of $1,000 helped to finance the O.C.E. (Operation—Cooperation Evangelism). This was the plan by which teams of students from our schools were sent out during the summer to minister in music and teaching and personal witness, in D.V.B. schools, camps, and youth work and in organized visitation for the local churches. With the discontinuance of O.C.E. as a home missions project, the $1,000 a year gift in 1967 and 1968 has helped the Home

Missions department in its sponsorship of work in Arizona and Hawaii.

Leadership of the Women's Missionary Society has always been of the highest quality and not least during this past decade, when the accomplishments have exceeded those of any previous ten-year period. Mrs. Willard Eckman's board, at the beginning of the past decade, consisted of leaders in local societies in the Nebraska churches. They met regularly, prayed earnestly, planned and worked diligently and achieved their goals during each of the years they served. During her four-year term Mrs. Eckman traveled approximately 26,000 miles during which time she visited all of the districts in which the Society had its membership.

Completing its four-year term in 1961, the Nebraska board turned over the leadership to an Eastern District board, with Mrs. Gustaf Erickson as president.

The Eastern board accepted the challenge of leadership and carried the program of the W.M.S. "onward and upward" toward still higher goals, exceeding the national project goals and increasing other aspects of missionary outreach. Mrs. Erickson, too, traveled thousands of miles visiting District societies in various parts of the country.

From the East coast, the leadership moved all the way to the West coast for the four-year period from 1965 to 1959, with Mrs. Reuben Strombeck as president and a board of dedicated and efficient co-workers from the southern California churches. Mrs. Strombeck has become the most traveled WMS president. Vacationing in Europe following her election in 1965, she sent her first greeting for the WMS page of the *Beacon* from there. In 1966 she visited our Venezuela mission field and wrote inspiring and illuminating articles about the work there. And last year (1968) she visited our mission fields in Japan, the Philippines, Hong Kong, Malaysia and Hawaii.

During her term an excellent "New Life Manual" was published, in loose-leaf form, containing a historical sketch of the Society entitled *Women at Work,* written by Mrs. Arnold Olson, plus the constitution of the Society; information on how to organize a WMS; how to lead the meetings; how to delegate responsibility, and helps on the conduct of an installation service. A section on Funds, another on Annual Projects, one on White Cross and another on Programs, along with brief biographies of the missionaries supported by the Society and short histories of each of the seven overseas mission fields in which the EFCA is working comprise the book, which appears to be an indispensable source of information not only for every WMS leader—local, regional or national—but for missionary candidates interested in specific fields.

A book of devotional meditations by Muriel Hanson, the gifted wife of President Calvin Hanson of Trinity Junior College, was introduced at the 1965 conference. A contest for the naming of the book had been sponsored by the WMS before its publication. Among the names submitted, *Honey and Salt* won the first prize.

Pondering as to what might be the secret of the unique success the Women's Missionary Society has had in all of its missionary endeavors, I reach the conclusion that the women have taken seriously not only the first word of their motto, but the second word as well, and that it is because of their continual emphasis on the *upward* aspect of their lives and work that their progress has been so definitely *onward,* year by year.

TWELVE

LAYMEN'S FELLOWSHIP

A FREE CHURCH LAYMEN'S FELLOWSHIP IS BORN

While the Women's Missionary Society of the Evangelical Free Church was observing its 60th anniversary during our general conference at Trinity last summer—when almost 1,000 women were present at the anniversary banquet—the new Free Church Laymen's Fellowship (FCLF) was in the process of becoming a permanent national organization, to take its place alongside the Women's Missionary Society, the Free Church Youth Fellowship and other branches of our Evangelical Free Church work.

Whether the FCLF will ever catch up with the WMS, which had such a head start, is something for the next decades to determine, but the fact that membership of the brand new organization was already at the 500-mark before the end of conference week is a pretty good indication that there is plenty of "vim, vision, vigor, and vitality" in the new men's organization.

The need of a men's organization had been sensed by leaders of the EFCA for some years before the organization took place.

The Executive Committee of the EFCA, in 1965, appointed a committee to consider the idea of a laymen's fellowship.

The Fellowship began to take shape during the 83d annual conference at Long Beach, California, in June of 1967. A program of very special interest to Free Church laymen had been planned as an attraction for the conference. Arrangements had been made for the men attending the conference to enjoy a half day of deep-sea fishing or a round of golf. There was a banquet with a special speaker. The main purpose, however, was to lay the ground work for an organization of laymen to further the work of the Lord in and through the Evangelical Free Church.

Moderated by Mr. J. Gordon Swanson of Central Free Church, Minneapolis, a one-day Laymen's Seminar was held on Wednesday of the conference, during which time four laymen led a discussion of four aspects of the work in which they were especially interested:

"The Laity and Evangelism"
"The Laity and Our Educational Institutions"
"The Laity and Pastoral Relationships" and
"The Laity and Its Relationship to Evangelical
    Free Church Affairs."

The afternoon session, moderated by Larry Strand, was devoted to planning, a discussion of purposes and objectives, and a presentation of the need of a men's organization. This resulted in a unanimous vote to form a national laymen's fellowship; an agreed-upon statement of purpose, and the formation of committees to establish objectives and prepare a resolution for presentation to the general conference.

The resolution presented to the conference—which had already been approved and recommended by the Executive Board—came up for consideration on Friday morning, and was approved by an enthusiastic and unanimous vote. It read: "We request authority of the 83rd annual conference of the Evangelical Free Church of America to establish an organization of Free Church laymen for the purpose of promoting the work of the Lord in and through the Evangelical Free Church of America."

The new FCLF was already "on its way," as our Beacon editor expressed himself following the conference. He also wrote, "The unbridled enthusiasm of the laymen was something .to behold. After two days they asked for permission to work on plans for setting up a men's organization and to report back to the 1968 conference for the final go-ahead sign."

A report on the progress of the preparations being made for the organization appeared in *The Evangelical Beacon* of December 5, 1967. The Steering Committee had met several times and had outlined its objectives more clearly, stated as follows:

(1) Promote support for our EFCA educational institutions.
(2) Promote personal evangelism.
(3) Promote good communication between ministerial and laity.
(4) Promote support of Shareholders projects.
(5) Help to develop leadership among laymen.

There was also a listing of several specific projects which the committee felt should have "immediate action." These included:

(1) Compilation of a minister's salary schedule.
(2) Offer assistance in study of Ministerial Pension Plan and Ministers Annuity and Aid Fund.
(3) Complete a mailing list of all Free Church laymen.
(4) Appoint a study group for radio and television.
(5) Establish an operational fund.

There was the appointment of a constitution committee, a program committee for the 1968 conference, a publicity and registration committee, a finance committee, and a committee to make local arrangements for the 1968 conference.

A representative for each of the 14 districts in the Evangelical Free Church was appointed. These would comprise the steering committee.

Publicity Chairman Robert Erickson of Des Moines reported on a meeting of the steering committee in Chicago on January 20, 1968, to lay further plans for the new organization and to discuss the 1968 conference to be held at Bannockburn in June. Men from Washington, Minnesota, Iowa, Illinois, Nebraska, and Connecticut were present. The first draft of the proposed constitution was read and discussed. Lapel emblems and designs were studied, and various committees reported to the group.

The permanent organization of the new Fellowship took place during the 1968 general conference following a day of lectures by Trinity professors, a series of panel discussions on pertinent subjects, and a luncheon meeting wtih Dr. John Swanson of Rockford as speaker.

Mr. Walter Govertsen of Trumbull, Conn., who had served so efficiently as temporary chairman since the 1967 conference, was elected the first president of the FCLF. Other members elected were: Robert Erickson of Des Moines, first vice president; Eugene High of Allentown, Pa., second vice president; Torry Froisland of Essex Fells, N.J., secretary; Herbert Nordin of Minneapolis, treasurer, and Arthur B. Hanson, Minneapolis, financial secretary.

The editor of the *Beacon,* commenting on the meeting, wrote, "New president Walter Govertsen has solid enthusiasm from all parts of the country backing him up as he guides this fledgling organization in the next year."

The constitution, with statement of purpose, membership, organization, officers, etc., was approved by the 84th general conference at the last business session of the conference, on Friday afternoon, June 21, 1968

With the blessing of the Lord and the blessing of the entire Evangelical Free Church constituency, there is reason to believe that our new Free Church Laymen's Fellowship will make a significant contribution to the work of the Lord and the Evangelical Free Church of America during the challenging days that lie ahead of us.

THIRTEEN

YOUTH FELLOWSHIP

NEW DIRECTION IN FREE CHURCH YOUTH FELLOWSHIP

The original purpose of the Free Church Youth Fellowship, organized in 1941, as stated by its organizer and first president, Mel Larson, was "to win souls, especially the young, for Christ, in the meantime furnishing a strong bond of Christian fellowship among the societies of our Evangelical Free Church."

Though this has continued to be the primary object of the organization, the first few years of its existence were characterized by a strong missionary emphasis, during which time they raised large sums of money to promote various missionary projects. They took on half-support for a missionary couple who had volunteered to go to Congo as missionary builders. They supplied a station wagon for the work in China, a three-ton truck for Congo, a truck for South America, a jeep for Kentucky, and a station wagon for our Free Church School in Chicago. A goal of $18,000 for home and foreign missionary work was set at their 1947 conference and a program calling for $24,000 was announced at their 1948 conference, at which time they were ready to call a full-time executive secretary to head up their work. They were still moving forward along these lines when they set their budget of $25,000 for the 1949-50 year.

Following the merger of the two Evangelical Free Church groups, in 1950, a shift of emphasis took place, or rather a return to the original purpose, broadened by a new statement in a revised constitution, setting forth the objectives of the organization as (1) to render assistance and aid to the local and district youth groups; (2) to unite Free Church youth in a bond of Christian fellowship and love; (3) to challenge our youth to consecrate their lives to Christ; (4) to encourage our young people to participate in the Free Church home and foreign missions program, and (5) to urge our young people to acquire a Christ-centered education.

Throughout the first decade of the merger (1950-1959), the FCYF accomplished its purposes by means of its annual conferences, provided a considerable amount of program material to the local youth groups, and maintained a weekly contact with them through the FCYF page in *The Evangelical Beacon*. Their annual projects were modest and not too difficult to attain while they worked to pay off a deficit that had accumulated during preceding years. At the end of the decade, at the beginning of the Diamond Jubilee Year of the Evangelical Free Church (January, 1959), Mel Larson made the comment that "The Free Church Youth Fellowship is carrying on a program based on service to the local youth societies."

This kind of service has been continued and stepped up during the past decade. It has included the devotional and inspirational material appearing on the FCYF page in the *Beacon;* a special youth magazine published for a few years, called *FCYF Focus;* a great deal of excellent program material supplied to the local groups; the promotion of Bible reading and Bible study, with practical suggestions and reading schedules; regional and national workshops and youth conferences, including the national FCYF conferences; encouraging and helping in the formation of Junior FCYF groups; contributing material for special Youth Week issues of the *Beacon,* the sending of an FCYF gospel team to visit the churches, etc.

They have also continued their special united projects during the past decade. They have continued to sponsor the Hilding Ahlstrom lectureship, which has brought to the campus of Trinity each year some outstanding Bible scholar or missionary statesman for a series of lectures. On several occasions substantial contributions have been made to the libraries of our schools, as well as scholarships for each of our three schools. Contributions have been made each year to *The Evangelical Beacon* as a token of appreciation for the FCYF page. Money was raised to bring to our country Luke Saba, the son of one of the first converts of the work in the Congo—a young minister working primarily with Congo youth. Their latest united project is to raise $3,000 to purchase a much-needed pick-up truck for Trinity Junior College, which they were hoping to present to the college this spring. This is called "Project Wheels."

One of the most popular programs the FCYF has sponsored during the past two or three years is the Bible Quiz program, in which local and regional FCYF teams compete against each other, according to rules prepared by the national FCYF. An exciting number on the program of our national Free Church conference last summer was the final contest between the two top teams— the one from McKeesport, Pa. and the team from Stanton, Nebraska. A quickened interest in our national conferences on the part of young people may be attributed to this new phase of the FCYF program.

Annual reports have been given by the president of FCYF each year until and including the conference of 1967. Since then, however, the work of the Free Church Youth Fellowship has been under the general direction of the Christian Education board, which has been re-organized to include not only Sunday school work but all youth activities. The Secretary of the Christian Education board is the executive director of the FCYF under the new program, and makes reports to the conference.

For several years the leaders of FCYF and those responsible for the Sunday School department have considered how they might improve *all* aspects of youth work in the Evangelical Free Church. They now believe the integration of the FCYF into the Christian Education department of the Evangelical Free Church of America will make for the general improvement of the entire youth program and a more effective ministry for Christ and our young people's work.

FOURTEEN

BENEVOLENT INSTITUTIONS

OUR BENEVOLENT INSTITUTIONS
EXPAND THEIR MINISTRY

While it has always been true that the Evangelical Free Church has given top priority to the command of our Lord to "make disciples of all nations," there has been from the very beginning of our work a concern for meeting humanitarian needs, such as caring for the orphans and for the aged. Four such institutions have been operated by the denomination for many years—two children's homes and two homes for senior citizens. A brief review of the ministry of these institutions during the past decade comprises this chapter.

However, this kind of Christian work, for the most part, is now being conducted by our District organizations, which at present own and operate no less than seven homes for senior citizens.

The North Central District owns and operates four such homes —the Elim Home of Princeton, the Elim Home of Milaca, the Elim Home of Watertown, all in Minnesota, and the Elim Home of Fargo, North Dakota.

The Great Lakes District has recently opened the beautiful new Fair Haven Christian Home in Rockford, Illinois.

The Maranatha Heights Home, in Lake Alfred, Florida, is owned and administered by the Southeastern District. The Pacific Northwest District operates a similar home at Port Townsend, Wash.

CHILDREN'S HOMES

The Christian Home for Children at Fort Lee, New Jersey, occupying a magnificent 7-acre site overlooking the Hudson River and Manhattan Island, near the west end of the George Washington Bridge, has ministered to between 70 and 90 homeless children during the past decade, receiving the loving care of Superintendent and Mrs. David Sunde and their efficient staff during this entire period until last year when they resigned and returned to Norway. The Rev. Robert Tonnesen assumed the superintendency as of May 1, 1968.

Throughout the 69-year history of the Home, the buildings have been kept in excellent condition, with additions and alterations made from year to year as needed.

The Home at Fort Lee is unique in that it consists of two homes—one for the winter months and one for the summer vacation months. The summer home at West Park, New York, where the boys and girls spend the entire summer vacation period, is well equipped to provide recreational and other facilities. In line with the policy of providing the best possible accommodations and facilities, a new building was erected on the summer campus two years ago to increase the capacity of the home.

The Lydia Children's Home, in Chicago, has done for homeless children in Chicago what the Fort Lee home has done in New York, providing a Christian home for some sixty boys and girls during the past decade.

After nine years of faithful and efficient service as superintendent, the Rev. Theodore DeBoer (whose tragic death took place on his way to our conference in Ocean Grove five years ago) left, in 1960, to assume a pastorate in Milwaukee. Following him as superintendent was the Rev. Gunnar Gunderson, who served for two years until the coming of the Rev. Carl Weir, who directed the work for five years, until 1967. The Rev. Irving Johnson, who had served as assistant superintendent for several years, took over as acting superintendent until December 1, 1968, when Chaplain Emmanuel Carlsen, who had served as chaplain in the Home for several months, became executive director and head of the Home.

As the 50th anniversary of Lydia was approaching, a campaign to raise $50,000 was launched for an addition to the present building. The golden jubilee banquet was held on October 14, 1966—a gala affair attended by hundreds of friends of Lydia.

Among the various methods of promotion employed by the Home, a quarterly magazine, *Life at Lydia,* has been published for many years, going to some 25,000 homes throughout the country and Canada.

SENIOR CITIZENS' HOMES

The Evangelical Free Church Home in Boone, Iowa, under the administration of the Rev. and Mrs. Arthur E. Anderson, has had a very successful decade, operating at full capacity year after year. The need for additional space and improved facilities was recognized ten years ago. When the Home observed its golden anniversary, in 1962, plans were in the making for the construction of a new wing which would include a nursing section. Ground was broken for the new addition on May 17, 1964, with dedication on June 13, 1965.

Since opening the new wing on July 1, 1965, the Home has been able to minister to almost twice as many residents, the average number in 1967 being 93.

The Andersons left on August 1, 1968, after presenting their 12th report to the conference at Trinity. In the meantime the Rev. Ernest J. Vick, who had pastored the Berean Evangelical Free

Church of Minneapolis, was called to superintend the Home. Mr. Vick took over as of September, 1968.

The Chrisian Homes of Holdrege, Nebraska, which had served for 65 years caring for homeless and dependent children, was converted into a home for senior citizens in 1955, when it became obvious that there was no longer a need for a children's home in that area. The Rev. Ivan Larson, who had served so well as superintendent of the Children's Home, became just as good a superintendent of the new Home, which had been remodeled to make the conversion possible.

In 1959 there were 59 residents in the Home, most of them Nebraskans. Operating at full capacity and with a waiting list for entrance, it was already obvious that there was need for an addition. Mr. Larson and the board of managers began to prepare plans for a 46-bed nursing wing to be connected to the north end of the present building. Succeeding the Rev. Ivan Larson, the new superintendent, Gordon R. Jensen, reported to the 1961 conference that the plans for the new addition had been approved and construction was expected to begin during that summer.

The nursing wing was completed the following summer and dedicated on October 21, 1962, just eight years after the conversion of the Home to a home for senior citizens. Fifty new residents were admitted the first year after the completion of the addition.

Since then there have been more than a hundred residents who have been cared for each year. As of conference time in 1968, a total of 134 had received care that year, with 107 in residence at the end of the year.

The Home observed its 80th anniversary (since the establishment of the children's home) on February 4, 1969.

Serving as chaplain at the Home is one of our veteran Evangelical Free Church ministers, the Rev. Oscar Anderson, who observed his 90th birthday last summer. He is the father of the Rev. Richard B. Anderson of our Congo field and of Dr. Herbert Anderson, director of the Conservative Baptist Foreign Missions Society.

FIFTEEN

TOMORROW'S HORIZONS

TOWARD NEW HORIZONS

We have been surveying the progress and expansion of the Evangelical Free Church during the past decade, considering each of the departments and institutions that comprise the whole. It might be well, in a concluding chapter, to present a brief summary of this progress before attempting to peer into the future and consider what role our denomination might fill in God's program during the next few years, if the Lord tarries.

Ten years ago there were 443 cooperating congregations. Today there are approximately 540. While the *number* of churches has not increased in the same proportion as during the preceding ten-year period, the total *church membership* has almost doubled during this period, with a total of close to 60,000, compared with the figure of 31,900 ten years ago. This indicates that there has been a considerable increase in the *size* of our churches.

Enrollment in the Sunday schools of the Evangelical Free Church has always exceeded that of the congregations. Five years ago our Sunday School department reported an enrollment of

70,000 in our schools. Our present secretary of Christian Education has indicated a 5.8% increase since 1966. Illinois, Minnesota and California rank highest in their Sunday school enrollment, with approximately 10,000 in each of these states.

The financial strength of our churches is almost three times what it was nine years ago, as indicated by the figure of $5,319,-732 in 1958-9 (total income to all churches) compared to $15,339,509 last year.

The spiritual impact of our Evangelical Free Church in our world cannot be measured by the size of the denomination. Our EFCA will continue to be one of the smaller religious bodies. What is significant is that there has been steady growth in every aspect of its program throughout the entire history of the denomination, and that it is being recognized by evangelicals around the world as a leading force in preserving and propagating "the faith once for all delivered unto the saints." Here are some of the spiritual resources which, placed at the disposal of the Lord, might well make the Evangelical Free Church of America a leader among the evangelical denominations of our country and Canada:

There is a zeal for making Christ known "to the uttermost part of the world" as evidenced by the fact that in per capita giving for overseas missions the Evangelical Free Church of America is at the very top of the list of denominations.

The theological seminary maintained by the denomination has become not only one of the fastest growing schools of its kind but a school that is recognized as one of the best in North America, attracting students from all over the world because of its outstanding faculty and sound evangelical convictions.

Many people outside the Evangelical Free Church have maintained that its denominational magazine, *The Evangelical Beacon,* is one of the best edited denominational magazines in North America, whose circulation is far in excess of many groups considerably larger in size.

Our denomination has provided leadership in many interdenominational organizations such as Youth for Christ, the Christian Business Men's Committee, the Evangelical Press Association, Inter-Varsity Christian Fellowship, the Evangelical Alliance Mission, the Billy Graham Evangelistic Association, etc. For a number of years the president of our denomination, Dr. Arnold T. Olson, has wielded a strong influence as a member of the board of the National Association of Evangelicals, of which he became president in April of 1968. He has also been active in the leadership of the International Federation of Free Evangelical Churches, whose headquarters are in Europe, and is the author of a history of that organization—*Believers Only*.

What role our Evangelical Free Church might have in the years to come, only God knows. The social revolution that is sweeping over the world, including our own country and Canada, is having its effect upon the Church as we have known it. There are gloomy predictions that "conventional Christianity" is destined to pass out of existence within the next generation, and that the Church will have to seek and find other ways of propagating the faith than the conventional methods of the past if it is to continue to justify its existence.

Concerned evangelicals are asking themselves such questions as "How can we stem the tide of lawlessness, violence, drug addiction, etc.? How far can we as evangelicals go in Social Action? Are we willing to make sacrifices of time, talents and resources as an expression of our social concern and commitment? Ought we to become involved as individuals in politics? Can we define the limits of the social implications of our Gospel?"

Resolutions adopted at the 26th annual conference of the National Association of Evangelicals, in April, 1968, make it clear that evangelicals are grappling with such problems and seeking solutions. They are frank to confess that

> while the evangelical church is awake to the problems of public morality and has a standard of Truth to present, it wavers in

the uncertainty of pluralism and relativism. This produces a whisper on moral issues that is too weak to call the Church to moral action. Inactivity is directly related to an "uncertain sound."

Evangelicals have not clearly defined the relationship between private and public morality. They are weak on the issues of public morality because they tend to be aligned with a middle class value system. They are uncertain about their role in public morality because of a weakened view of the end of history.

The Committee on Christian Social Concern of our Evangelical Free Church, reporting to our 1968 conference last summer, declared that "the Church must speak to public moral issues with the New Testament priorities of meeting human needs and preserving human rights, and must commend and support any agency —spiritual or secular, public or private—which is following such priorities, and should condemn the failure of a society to meet such needs . . . The Church must adopt a concept of Christian witness that includes public influence as well as personal evangelism."

In his annual report to the 1968 annual conference, President Arnold Olson reminded us that "We face what may well become the most trying year in missions abroad, evangelism at home, and in higher education. We may have to face more difficult decisions in one year than in the previous decade." Among other things, he asked for authority to arrange a special summer session for the study of methods for approaching the problems of the inner city and the race question. I quote from his report:

This would be done together with a selected number of evangelical denominations with similar problems and emphases. The teachers would be chosen mostly from among those actually engaged in such work rather than theoreticians. Preliminary discussions are already under way with a few interested denominational leaders. The summer sessions would be open to our pastors who are concerned enough and can give a part of a summer in coming to grips with such problems.

Concluding that portion of his report, he declared, "The time has come for us to move from the mercy seat where we confess our sins to the places outside the camp where we bear His reproach."

As we face these problems in the future and seek solutions, it is good to remind ourselves of the Master Builder of the Church, who declared that "The gates of hell shall not prevail against it," and of the promise to His disciples that, as they obeyed the Great Commission, He would be with them, "always, even unto the end of the age."

The Macedonian call, "Come over and help us," is being heard and answered by our mobile generation while it views more of the landscape from land, sea and air than any previous inhabitants of planet earth. The cry is heard from many geographically and spiritually changing old horizons in rural and urban North America and in nations around the world, as well as in places where new Evangelical Free churches dot the horizon. This need will abide and God's presence will remain with us as we continue blessedly involved in the work of the gospel, wherever He may lead . . . until we are caught up at Christ's appearing to utterly new horizons, and the present scene is replaced with new heavens and new earth, as He promised.